STOP

IGNORING ME

THE CRY OF MY HEART

ROZ HUMPHREYS

Cover Design Credits: Richard Perez
Interior Photography Credits: Tina Pirozzoli
Book Formatting: www.bookclaw.com

ISBN-13:978-0-692-95338-9

ISBN-10:0-692-95338-8

For Bulk Ordering or Distribution, please contact author at
www.rozhumphreys.com

For the women of my
Past, Present and Future of
Inspiration and Influence

Table of Contents

Introduction

Have you ever had one of those days when you wanted to scream or just run away? The dishes are piled up, your children are cranky, dinner is late and your husband won't be home for hours. Maybe you're a single mom or have recently been faced with the care of an elderly parent. Wherever you are in life, I'm sure, at one time or another, you've day dreamed yourself away from the chaos. In your dream, you leave everything behind and enter into a quieter time in your past or in your future where you envision fewer demands that would allow you to just "be." Maybe, like many of us, you have held onto this dream because in the quest to serve others, you have ignored yourself.

As a Latina, I know the burden and reward that my culture places on the role of women in the care of loved ones. In today's world, women have been labeled as superwomen and many crumble under the immense pressures of taking on all the care-giver responsibilities. They silently die to self. Women push aside self as a priority and pour everything they have into those they love. Unfortunately, everyone else's needs become a priority.

As you know, women are multifaceted. They take on roles like daughters, sisters, wives, aunts, mothers and grandmothers, business women, entrepreneurs, chair persons; the list can go on and on. These roles help define who she is. However, in the process of fulfilling those roles, the inner gal gets lost. The gal outside is all smiles, but the girl within cries and wonders where she has gone wrong -- why she is not fulfilled -- especially when she's doing what's expected.

If the woman inside of you could get your attention for one moment, what would she ask you? What does she crave, wish, hope and pray for? Would you listen intently and lovingly? Think about it, if you can't treat yourself lovingly and with intention, how are you going to be your best for others? Yet you and I do this every day.

Introduction

Too many of us have chosen to ignore ourselves and our dreams because we are overwhelmed with our other roles and the demands that life has placed on us. We neglect our needs and wear our neglect as a badge of sacrifice. Unfortunately, that badge eventually sticks its needle right into the most precious part of our being; our heart. There is no escaping this. If you have not yet felt the piercing pain of neglect, it will happen sooner than later.

STOP IGNORING ME was designed to purposely guide you through a must-take journey that will help you get the type of life you've desired for so long. You will learn how to be kind to yourself...first. Kindness to self is one of the key factors to experience healing. Why is that so important? Your healing process cannot start, proceed, or continue until your kindness focus becomes a priority in your life. It requires a lot of work, and the work will be worth it because, at the end of the journey, you will find inner-peace and true fulfillment in order to live the life you have always desired.

This book will give you the tools you need to help you say:

1. I will live a happier and longer life.
2. I will impact my kids, grand babies, and other women in my life as a positive role model.
3. I will follow my heart and make my dreams a reality.

Perhaps you feel undeserving due to soul wounds from your past or because of the lack of self-esteem. Let me reassure you that all of us have had our self-esteem compromised at one point or another. What's important is that you take a good hard look and find ways to fix those areas of your life that you have given up on. This guide will help you discover, uncover, and repair many areas and will explore the following questions.

1. Are you living authentically or as a carbon copy?
2. How much time do you invest into worry and fear?
3. Are you really insecure or are just facing self-doubt?
4. How good are you as a person?
5. Are your choices giving you what you want?
6. Are your friends helping you become your best?
7. Does your heart really matter?

There is no timeline in completing this journey. However, it is important that you do not rush through the book; do not skip or skim because you'll miss vital information; and do not forget or avoid completion of any homework at the end of each chapter. There is also a free, downloadable workbook on my website that provides indepth exercises and activities for each chapter..

Remember, this is about you; no one else. I believe you can begin and complete this journey. I also believe that in your decision to pick up this life-changing book, you have already taken the first step.

Welcome to the beginning of a new life!

How to Use This Book

- Are you committed to yourself?
- Do you take the time to really get to know yourself?
- Do you practice care, love and appreciation towards yourself?

Did you know there's nothing wrong with doing any of the above?

If your answer to any of these questions made you feel uncomfortable, it may be because your nurturing qualities have been more outward than inward. Let me share a secret with you. You cannot be an effective nurturer, lover, friend, leader, mentor, etc., unless you are well-rounded in body, soul and spirit. So with that in mind, I challenge you to begin your journey to <u>explore and accept</u> who you are. Be brutally honest. Don't cheat or short-change yourself. Take a deep dive into your own heart and believe that this is your time to heal and change. You are worth every step.

The format of the book is consistent throughout. Each section includes a…

Reflection
Introduction
Story
Lesson
Assignment

The **Reflection** sections have thought-provoking poems or small essays for meditation designed to prepare your heart and mind for the upcoming lesson. The **Introduction** will present what is being covered in the chapter and will open the forum for the story.

The **Story** covers the lives of four women, Aggie, Dee, Leena, and Ellie. Their lives are intertwined and each story is designed to highlight and demonstrate the subject matter covered in the chapter. Certain words are highlighted in bold throughout the story. These words will help you identify, relate, and focus on those key areas in your own life.

A **Lesson** follows each story and is designed to lead you to discover what you need to change, add, or remove from your life.

Each chapter ends with an **Assignment**. The Assignment will help you reinforce what you have learned and will require an action from you.

There is an accompanying workbook on my website (www.rozhumphreys.com) that provides more in-depth assignments that correlate with each chapter. It is optional. However, it is an additional tool that you can use in your journey to become your authentic and better you.

If you choose not to add the workbook, I encourage you to start a journal. Write down your thoughts as you read the Reflections. As you read the Story, write down the words that strike a chord within you. As you proceed through the Lesson, write down what you've learned about yourself or what has impressed you the most and may need further thought or meditation.

Also, in the Assignment phase, be sure to write down what you're committed to and keep track of your progress. If you need accountability, invite a friend to walk this journey with you.

Take your time. This journey should not to be rushed. Pace yourself and enjoy life's wonderful heart-changes within you.

Behind the Mask of Hurt

Masked Heart

Behind a masked heart, all remains hidden
Outward smiles painted with hues of laughter
Deceived awareness covering the intense
Disarray of one whom stands alone

The curse of joy that's freely given
To those who need or will receive
And yet the inner being is quite misleading
Of this display of inner peace

There is inside a bitter longing
For this charade to have an end
Perhaps display the depth and substance
A valued heart you are my friend

Mask Introduction

Ever want to curl up inside yourself and just disappear? I think all of us have felt that at one time in our lives. These feelings can be triggered by experiences like a loss (sudden death of a relative or friend), expectations that were not met (a relationship that did not work), hurtful words or actions (a fight with a spouse, parent or sibling), or by a memory (childhood abuse or unforgiveness). These types of negative emotions cause you to disappear or hide behind all kinds of masks. The formation of these masks happens as a result of perceptions that you have shaped or are shaped by what you believe others have told you. You create and redesign these masks again and again and do not even realize it. Your thoughts about yourself, your belief about what others think about you, and your own desire to be accepted, all play a part in the creation of the masks you hide behind.

Your internal dialogue plays an important part on how you view yourself in the present and the future. The mind has an incredible way to retrieve past experiences and past perceptions you think you have hidden. Smells, music and certain words can trigger sensations and memories long forgotten. Even though you may think you have buried these memories or thoughts, they can come back to you in an instant - whether pleasant or painful. And when they do come back, they threaten to overwhelm your mind with fresh pain and that causes you to hide, once again, behind another mask.

The following story will help you better understand how masks are formed, how they are used and how they cause damage in your life.

Mask Story

It had been close to six months since they've last seen each other. Life's busy schedule had kept them apart. Aggie decided to break the pattern by enticing them to a day filled with pampering that would include lunch, facials, manicures, pedicures, and her famous, mouth-watering, home-made cheesecake. She knew that her cousin, Ellie and closest friends, Dee and Leena, wouldn't be able to resist.

Aggie sat in the living room with the girls after lunch. They talked, laughed and relived old memories as they often did when they were together. However, it was par for the course that one of them would start egging the other. You know how it goes with close friends and family; there are just some things that they'll never let you live down.

"Remember when you used to babysit me? You were really mean when we were growing up." Ellie teased.

"I wasn't mean!" yelled Aggie as she threw a pillow across the room towards her cousin Ellie. Laughter rang out after both remarks.

"Do you remember the time when I was **not allowed** to be part of the club you all had? What was the reason? Ah yes, I was the youngest."

"Poor Ellie, what's the matter…still **feel left out**?" chided Aggie.

"Gosh, yes. I would've done anything to be part of it. Thinking about it still makes me mad."

"Not as mad as when what's-her-name **took** Jay **away** from you." Leena's eyes twinkled with mischief.

"Ah, you had to go there!" Ellie yelled. The laughter became a roar accompanied by the usual hand clapping and peels of small screams.

"**Talk about rejection,**" Ellie said with a sarcastic tone and hint of humor.

Dee caught the last part of the conversation as she walked into the living room. "Gosh if rejection was always that simple, life would be cake," Dee chimed in.

"How can you say that?" Leena's smile became a frown and before anyone else could get a word in otherwise she continued. "Do you realize what rejection does and how it changes you in a hurtful way?"

"Oh, stop being such a drama queen," Ellie quipped.

Dee jumped in as she responded to Ellie, "Wait, she has a point there. I mean, I remember how **devastated** you were and how **depressed** you got when Jay left you."

Ellie looked past Dee as if lost in her own memories. Her face wrinkled with fresh pain. "You know for a long time I felt **lost, ugly,** and **crushed.** I found myself **second guessing my looks,** and for a while, I was really **afraid** to start over because I did not want to get **hurt again.**"

"Hmm, I could understand that." Dee reached over and put her arms around Ellie.

"At least you didn't live with a man for ten years who **neglected** you. Now that's rejection." All of them turned to look at Leena. Her angry tone caught them by surprise.

"I have lived a very **lonely** life for the past 10 years," Leena continued, "and because of it, I **no longer trust** any man. He made me feel **undesirable** and his constant absence made me feel **forgotten** and **not valued.** I couldn't change my situation for a long time because I felt **powerless, unable to choose.** Unbelievable…right? Why? Because **I believed that I didn't deserve** to be happy. You see when you live as many years as I have filled with rejection, **you start to believe all the negative voices in your head.** For a long time **I felt it was my fault**."

A sob escaped from her lips and everyone froze and stared in disbelief. Leena and her husband seemed happy. Some of them had mentioned in passing conversations how he seemed a bit over-protective of her, but none had seen or heard anything to have caused any of their flags to go up.

"Why didn't you tell us?" Aggie blurted out when she found her voice.

"I can't believe you kept this quiet. My gosh Leena, we could've helped you," Ellie said quietly as tears filled her eyes.

Leena put her head down, not wanting to meet any of their eyes. "I didn't know how to tell anyone." Her voice cracked.

Dee engulfed her in a warm embrace. Leena looked up and with a sad smile she continued to explain. "When we first got married, I thought I could change him. I thought if he loved me enough, he would change. I knew he was a bit over-protective but, I saw it as his wanting to keep me safe. He started to criticize almost everything I did, whether it was how I cooked, cleaned, or dressed. Every time I tried to defend myself, he would lash back at me so harshly. I started to back down to keep the peace. After hearing the same things over and over again, I started to feel **inadequate**."

Ellie walked over and grabbed her chin, "But hon, how could you believe that?"

"Ellie, when someone tells you something over and over again, you **start to question if you can do anything right and even question who you are. You start to believe what is said after a while.**" She paused and continued in a choked whisper, her eyes brimming with tears, **"You actually start to believe all the negative things you're told,** and what's worse is that **you begin to accept** that perhaps **that's who you truly are."**

After a long pause, Dee was the one to finally break the silence.

"Leena, I had no idea." She looked around and continued, "I don't think any of us did." Everyone nodded in unison.

"I hid it well. **I hid behind my clown mask** -- always smiling on the outside. I felt like **I had to keep everyone happy**, like **I had**

to keep a happy appearance. I felt like I was silently dying inside because I **had to keep quiet and keep how I really felt a secret**."

"But why did you think you had to be quiet, Leena? And what do you mean about hiding behind a mask?" Aggie's face showed genuine concern and hurt for her dear friend.

"We all wear masks at one time or another, Aggie. We interchange them depending on the situation or person we deal with. The longer you wear the mask, the safer you think it makes you feel. My mask **made me believe that I was happy when I wasn't**. Whenever you're not true to who you are, you're wearing a mask."

"But why bring it up now? What happened?" Aggie pushed further.

"What happens to every woman? You get to the point where you can only take so much. Something just snaps inside, and you know it's time to change and do what's good for you. I got tired of feeling depressed and was even more tired of living a lie. I smile on the outside and cry on the inside. It gets old after a while. It was time to stop wearing the mask and begin being myself."

Mask Lesson

Perhaps one of the worst feelings anyone can relate to is that of rejection. Rejection comes in a lot of different ways but the outcome is the same. It always brings pain. It can be subtle or it can be blatant and devastating. One thing is for sure, rejection causes deep hurt that can be felt immediately, can haunt you mercilessly, or can creep up on you years later when you least expect it.

The story began with a memory. It started with Ellie's recollection of not being allowed into Aggie's club. Although brought up in jest, the feelings of rejection were still real and raw. The memory dredged up feelings and caused Ellie to relive the anger she felt from this rejection. Most people can get past childhood experiences, but sometimes a person may bring up certain events over and over again because it still bothers them.

The next example in the story was again in the past, and was an experience that most of us have been through -- the heartache of a break up. What does that have to do with you now? Stay with me, we'll get there soon.

Everyone has felt the sting of rejection, especially during the dating years. What do you believe happens with each new rejection experience? What do you sense happens when this action repeats itself over and over again?

Leena was able to articulate some of those feelings. She felt **undesirable, forgotten, not valued, powerless,** and **blamed herself**. She recognized what was happening from the very beginning, but did not seek help and waited ten years before she decided to share anything. Perhaps you can empathize with her.

Did you notice that Ellie's memory of her rejection caused Leena's old pain to surface and allowed her to finally voice her pain after so many years? Did you wonder why she was afraid to say anything during the time she was going through her experience of rejection? Perhaps she was trying to protect herself, her husband, their/his/her reputation. Maybe her decision to keep up the appearance of a good marriage was based on her upbringing, beliefs or culture or the concern of what others thought about her?

Although you know that it is not a bad thing to share how you feel inside to those closest to you, there are instances when you just don't want to say anything at all in fear of sounding like a broken record or in fear of being rejected because of your feelings. So you do what most do. You put on a mask and hide the hurt in your heart. A mask can be worn for a very long time before anyone discovers the truth and what is behind the mask. Usually, by the time this happens, there's a lot of damage because of what lies underneath. You have conditioned yourself to cover how you truly feel inside. It shows up as anger or despair. It manifests as deep depression, but often it is hidden behind laughter. You smile on the outside and cry on the inside.

Would you agree that you cannot control what someone says? Did you know, however, that *you can* control how you react to what is being said? You can dismiss or embrace it. When you choose to embrace negative words or actions from others, you also choose to reinforce them within yourself. You add them to your belief system about yourself. However, you have a choice. Think of it this way. You have the power to choose to accept and embrace a negative word or action, *and* you also have the power to choose what your reaction will be to it.

You possess the power of choice. You exercise it every day. You decide whether to get up, get dressed, go to work, stay home, etc. Young or old, limited or not, you still possess the ability to choose.

Do you know that you also have the power to choose whether or not you talk yourself into or out of hurt? You have the potential to continue to nurture your hurt because of the choice to reinforce your internal, negative-dialogue. Whether it is a reaction to something said or done if it's because you beat yourself up mercilessly, you alone did the choosing; no one else.

Perhaps your negative dialogue sounds something like the following examples for certain situations? Learn to counteract them with truths that are wholesome and will build you up.

The following pages have some examples. The format begins with the:

1. Description of an emotion or situation
2. A negative, internal-dialogue
3. An internal, counteract-dialogue
4. Positive actions that can be taken

These steps will teach you how to apply positive changes to real-life, undesirable situations.

Emotion:
I feel lonely but I'm not going to tell or show anyone.
Those closest to me should sense how lonely I feel.

Negative:
Nobody loves me.

Counteract:
I have friends and family who love me and care about my feelings.

Positive A:
You are loved and are never alone.

Do not hide how you feel; especially if you feel hurt.

Pick up the phone, email or write and get in touch with someone close to you. People cannot read your mind, and true friends will always be there for you, and will nurture you when needed. Tell them you're feeling a little blue and alone and need some loving. Take it a step further and look up a friend or family you haven't spoken to for a while.

Reminisce, make a date to meet, and be consistent by staying in touch with those who love you. Do it now. Remember, you are loved. Reach out and let others in your life know how much you love them.

Positive Actions will always shut down
masked feelings and dialogues,
and will help you keep things in perspective.

Situation:
I don't like the way my body looks and I make fun of myself when I'm around my slim friends. It helps me hide how I truly feel about myself.

Negative:
I'm so fat; it's disgusting.

Counteract:
I'm a little overweight and will care for myself a bit better.
(Note: Okay maybe you're a lot over, but stop being so harsh. So what, you've got a little here and there. Hellooooo, most of us do!)

Positive A:
Your beauty begins inside of you.

If you are unhappy about your weight, do not hide behind the comfort of food.

Start to eat healthy and start to move. Join a gym. If you can't, search online, or find a live-stream workout program or download an app. You'll be surprised what 30 minutes of "moving" can do for you. Walk. Better yet, get a friend to walk with you. Stop making excuses and do what's "good" for you. I don't believe in diets. It's better to make a lifestyle change. Eat healthy and move. It'll change you; trust me.

Positive Actions will always shut down
masked feelings and dialogues
and will <u>instill a caring-attitude for you</u>.

Situation:
My phone hasn't rung all day. I'm not going to tell him that I was crying all day. I don't want to seem insecure.

Negative:
He doesn't care about me anymore. He has lost interest in me.

Counteract:
I'm going to call him so I don't make any assumptions. He is probably busy and hasn't had the time to call.

(Note: Men's thoughts are like drawers. They can only open one at a time. Ladies let me let you in on a little secret. Men are not like us. We are multitask queens.)

Positive A:
You are a queen (and I say that sincerely because that is what you are).

Weigh what is important to you.

Learn not to hide behind assumptions. What are your expectations? When you are sure you've identified what you want or need, set a time to communicate that to your partner. They are not mind-readers. You won't receive anything you don't ask for, and you should never assume they know what you want. Men and women think and process differently.

If you want something in life, you need to learn how to ask and not nag, be disrespectful or vague. You must be direct. If you truly cared for yourself, you would ask for a want or need instead of meeting others wants and needs "all the time." I can hear some of you now. "I can't help it. I'm a nurturer!"

Wouldn't you be an even better nurturer if you lived a balanced and fulfilled life, and not have to sweat his not calling you?

Positive Actions will always shut down
masked feelings and dialogues,
and will set the correct level of expectations.

What have you noticed? **Most times you will feed an emotion from a lie that you've made truth.** This becomes a vicious cycle. You and you alone, are responsible when it comes to the reinforcement of your dialogues of lies. Does that mean words or actions do not hurt? Of course they do, however, you have the power to feed or starve any hurt. What happens when you feed a plant? It will grow and flourish. What happens if you don't? It will wither and die.

When you feed your own internal, negative-dialogue, you're actually maintaining your detrimental excuses. Excuses, in turn, fuel your need to wear masks. Masks do not allow you to deal with what hurts you. Instead you opt to hide. You hide how you truly feel, hide your faults, hide your fears, and hide anything that may be viewed as negative or unacceptable. The lie you live becomes truth not only to you, but to others as well.

So how do you break this bad pattern?

What do you think helped Leena start healing? Would you agree that her first step to heal was to identify the specific areas that hurt her? Once any problem, issue, or in this case, hurt is identified, you're faced with the choice of acknowledgement. In reality, most of us know what our hurts are, but for some reason we won't acknowledge how much we hurt. We'd rather avoid the hurt or dismiss how we feel.

Let's stop here and let's take some time to explore.

Perhaps there are some areas in your life that need to be addressed. Why don't you take some time to answer the following questions? Who better to be honest with, than with yourself?

No More Mask Assignment

You wear a mask when you feel there is a need to hide the real you. It's important to be the real, bona fide you.

- List the areas where you may be wearing a mask.
- Make a commitment to get rid of one mask starting today.

Choose a piece of jewelry that will remind you of your commitment to lose one mask and live authentically. DO NOT take off that piece of jewelry (under any circumstance) until you've gotten rid of that mask.

REPEAT as often as needed, but do only one mask at a time!

Masks quiet down and hide the fears that we refuse to face.

Inward
Run

You Can't Run

How can you run
when there's no place to hide
Your mind is screaming
look deep down inside

You say you must change
the world you live in
The things that oppress you
you're caving within

But there is an answer
that most do ignore
A key that will open
a door, I implore

If just for a moment
you acknowledge you can't
Surrender your heart
and give life a chance

Then answers will straighten
the chaos inside
For when love takes over
the running subsides

Inward Run Introduction

Have you heard of the professional procrastinator? It's a person who puts off doing things on a consistent basis, such as paying bills, making phone calls, studying for a test, etc. It is difficult for a procrastinator to accomplish certain tasks in a timely manner. I'm sure you know a few. Some might say that they do this because they're trying to run away from their responsibilities. However, if you would ask any of them why they procrastinate, they'll probably tell you that it's just a nuisance to do certain things. The procrastinator may even add, "What's the rush? It'll get done."

The emotional runner is a lot like the procrastinator. All of us, at one point or another, procrastinate. We all run away from certain things within our lives for one reason or another. We avoid tackling certain problems or issues, facing uncomfortable situations, or standing up for what we believe in. Perhaps most of us do this because we hope it will all go away. Let's face it. Our natural instinct is to believe that if we ignore something long enough, it'll disappear and resolve itself. We numb it, shelve it, and convince ourselves that it is forgotten. Reality is that anything that remains unresolved will resurface. Whether it's now or years from now on a sick bed, during a crisis, during a depression, or on your exit from this earth, the issue will come back. Unresolved issues, no matter what they are, will always manifest themselves in our lives physically, emotionally, mentally, and spiritually.

Let's hone in on one of the ladies' lives that we've met in the last chapter, and take a peek through her life-window. You may find she sounds a lot like you.

Inward Run Story

Dee was always the quiet one of the group, but her display of love and compassion for others spoke volumes. Right before Leena left, she pulled Dee to the side and expressed her thanks. If you recall, Dee held Leena during the whole time she shared her ordeal. Her quiet support helped beyond words.

The get-together ended with an upbeat note and renewed dedication to their relationships. They promised that they would make it a point to stay in touch more often, and vowed to be more available to one another. All the gals left the house feeling Leena's hurt and a twinge of guilt. However, they also walked away with new insight when it came to the importance and frailty of friendship.

Ellie offered to give Dee a ride home, but she declined. Instead, Dee asked that she be dropped off at the railroad. During the train ride home, Dee replayed the conversation that unfolded amongst her friends that day. She started to think about her own life and struggles. She was a single mother of a five-year-old boy. Her husband had passed away three years earlier of a sudden heart attack. He was taken at a young age; a statistic of the killer, stress. His passing forced her to reenter the work force. She chose a practical line of business that was enjoyable to her and would allow her certain flexibilities that the corporate world would not afford her.

The location of her job, La Casita, also known as the "Little House" was in Queens, New York. The hair salon catered to anyone that walked through its doors and had a steady stream of clientele. All of Dee's coworkers were treated like family except for her. They knew about each other's lives, celebrated their children's birthdays together, swapped trade-secrets, amongst many other things. Dee, however, **didn't ever feel like she fit in.** She always believed that she had to work hard to **try to earn their acceptance.** This need drove her to make a risky decision - one that was completely out of character for Dee. She decided to share the intimate conversation of her get-together with her co-workers. Dee relayed in great detail the conversation they had. Unfortunately, she was met with a reaction she didn't expect.

"So you're telling me that **she lived miserably for 10 years with this man and didn't say a word?**" Her boss' grimace made Dee uncomfortable.

"Well, she explained that when you're told something over and over again, you begin to believe it. She was **afraid of what people would think.** They always looked happy." Dee's voice trailed off.

"Hmmm," Wilma's scrutiny increased her uneasiness. "So what advice did you give your girlfriend to help her with this mess?"

Dee went stone silent, **feared the worst**, and then began to stammer. "I didn't need to give her advice. Everyone else did."

Wilma looked exasperated and began to give Dee an earful of what *she* would have said. "First of all, I would've told her that a true friend should not be afraid of telling other friends their problems." **Dee cringed**. Wilma continued. "If I was her, I would have kicked him to the curb! And you didn't say anything?"

Dee shook her head no, **avoiding eye contact** knowing there was a lot more to come. The final blow arrived with, "What kind of friend are you?"

Dee escaped further interrogation by volunteering to do highlights on a woman's hair across the floor of the salon. As she began to put the woman's hair in foil, Dee felt **regret.** She shouldn't have said anything, she thought to herself. She just **didn't like conflict**, even if her **defense meant her silence.** Dee knew there was a time and a place for everything, but for some reason **she felt**

intimidated by others, more than she cared to admit. She **despised her weakness.** She comforted herself by ending her thoughts with "Hey they don't know the real me." Dee knew her actions spoke louder than words. That was her gift.

After Dee left work, she started to **beat herself up** once again. She felt **angry and depressed.** "Serves me right," she told herself. "**I got what I deserved.**" Her internal dialogue continued, "I should have stood up for Leena. I know why she did what she did." She sighed deeply and screamed inside "Why am I **so unsure** of myself? What in the world am I **scared** of? Maybe, I'm scared to admit that I knew how she felt because I went through the same thing with David before he died. My gosh, how can I taint his memory like that? What am I thinking?"

❧

Dee was glad to be off the next day. She decided to take her son to see her dad, a retired postal worker. Although she loved her father dearly, she always **felt like he was disappointed in her.** As she grew older, she noticed that he began to share his heart often, giving her insights on the why he did certain things. Her dad happened to be in one of those moods when she arrived.

"You know Dee," Herman began, "I am the proudest man in the world. You turned out to be a beautiful and successful woman."

Dee looked at her father with **sarcastic disbelief.** "Dad, come on. Rachel and Johnny have both finished college, they have great jobs, make lots of money, and both have houses. **Me? Look at me. I am not as successful** as they are."

Her father smirked then grinned. "Is that what you think success is?"

Dee let out a loud sigh.

"Do you love what you do?"

"Why are you asking that?" Dee **became defensive**.

He gently repeated, "Dee, do you love what you do for a living?"

She answered in frustration "Of course I do!"

"Do you love your son and being a mother?" he pushed further.

Dee grew impatient. "Yes, daddy I love being a mom."

"Success should not be measured by how much education you have, what type of job or home you have, what kind of car you drive, or clothes you wear. Do you know how many people I know that had all of those things and were unhappy?"

As if reading her mind, he continued, "No honey, those are all material things. What's inside of you is what holds worth and value. Take it from your old man. I've lived a long time and have seen lots of things. True success is doing what you love most and being 'your' best at it. It's knowing who you are, realizing your purpose, and recognizing your value as a giver to all that cross your path."

Dee couldn't help but think of Leena. She decided it was time to be honest with her father.

"**I always felt guilty** because I didn't finish college. **I beat myself up mercilessly** because I am afraid that **I will never measure up** in your eyes."

"Ah Dee," her father held her at arm's length and looked into her eyes. "Forget college. You don't have to prove anything to me, because in my eyes you have surpassed all my expectations."

Dee felt a heavy burden lift off her shoulders. She wished she had talked to her dad sooner.

Inward Run Lesson

Have you ever watched any of the shows that challenge a person to face their fears? Well if you haven't, the contestants are faced with some hair-raising challenges. If, for example, you're scared of heights, the show will provide an exercise that will make you face that fear. The contestants are expected to complete the challenge or crumble under the pressure. In the show, the person purposely puts themselves in a position to overcome their specific fear. Of course, it helps to know that the reward for winning is money. What would you do if you were given the opportunity to do the same, except the challenge would be to tackle your fears with a guaranteed reward? Would you do it?

Fear is an emotion that can deform a person's emotional state. It can drop the bravest to their knees, make the strongest whimper, and make the healthiest weak. Did you know that your emotional state has a direct impact on your health? Look at any woman that is going through some major stress, and you'll see that she either has a trail of (unwanted) zits, has gained a few pounds or looks like a raccoon (dark circles under the eyes). I know. I've been there! Now you're probably saying, what does stress have to do with fear? Stress is another word for anxiety. Anxiety is caused by tormenting thoughts because of, you guessed it, fear.

Would you agree that all of us have certain weaknesses in our lives that make us uncomfortable? What do you think Dee was afraid of? Perhaps she felt that she would have been ridiculed, maybe even chastised if she spoke up? Have you ever been in that type of situation? We probably have all been at one time or another and have opted to keep quiet, rather than create waves. I'm sure you have heard the saying, be slow to speak but quick to listen. However, what do you think happens when you repeatedly repress what you truly want to say because you are afraid of what others may think, or because you fear that your words may come back to haunt you? This type of censor can eventually take its toll and imprisons you in your own mind. **You scream on the inside, and express how you truly feel, but no one can hear you because your expressions have become a silent cry.**

It will come as no surprise to you that you are your own worst critic. Your internal dialogue reinforces hundreds of thoughts that cross your mind daily. You choose to dismiss them, or to accept them. Do you think that her best friends would've been supportive if she had admitted her marriage relationship difficulties? Who knows, perhaps it would've helped Leena to see that she was not alone in her experience. Why do you think that Dee is so afraid to express her hurts? Maybe she was traumatized when she was younger? Maybe she never felt good enough among her siblings? No doubt, the loss of her spouse was a devastating experience. Her frustrations and her fears haunted her and made her second-guess herself constantly. **Sometimes, a real life fear, in one part of your life, can become a false perception that you carry into all the areas of your life.**

Fear causes you to run inward. You formulate the belief that running takes you to a safe place, when in reality, it imprisons you. It fills you with assumptions (false beliefs) that you accept as reality. It fills you with doubt and creates insecurities. Would you agree that running is not the answer? How many times have you run away from the people who hurt you or from the problems that you face? Think about it, in actuality, you are running from you. In any case, sooner or later, the run has to stop. When that happens, it forces you to muster up all your courage so you can look at your hurt square in the eye. You then have to evaluate whether the fear you're experiencing is real or not and, if it is, choose to overcome it.

Fear has been sometimes defined as False Expectations Accepted as Real. The key word here is *false*. When was the last time you assessed those uncomfortable areas of your life? You know the one that brings dread to your heart. Keep this in mind. **Fear is a**

warden, a thief, and a cynic. It will imprison you because of your past; it will rob you of your present; and it will plant the seed of doubt that eventually takes root and chokes any and all future possibilities.

However, not all fear is bad. There is good fear. The 'don't touch-the-stove-because-it's-hot' kind of fear. This type of fear has a protective factor and helps you discern certain situations. For example, if the junk yard dog who happens to be a jaw locker gets loose and is growling and heading towards you, fear gets you moving! If you come home late one night and you hear footsteps, what is your first reaction? You pick up the pace because your instincts kick in and tell you, speed up, get away, and protect yourself! Again, fear is not all bad. However, there needs to be a healthy balance.

The fear that is being defined in this chapter is harmful, clouds judgment, is evil and keeps you trapped. Fear can take many shapes and forms. For example, it may look like a guardian who protects your heart when it actually shuts you in and everyone else out. Fear will lie to you every time. It will state that you have an iron heart when in reality it has numbed you to all possibilities, both towards your present and future. Fear will manifest through defensive attitude. It will hide the real reason for your sadness, anger, resentment, bitterness, loneliness, etc. Unlike the good fear, hurtful and false fear leaves no room for reason nor will it allow you to be sensitive. The beauty of sensitivity is that it forces you to feel. A soul-ache is an indication that something is out of sync and needs to be fixed. You can't heal if you refuse to feel.

Are you tired of living trapped by fear? If so, let's break free from the fear that is detrimental. It's time.

The first step is to identify those areas. Once you know what you're dealing with, you can begin to change. Let's look at a few examples in the next few pages.

Situation:
I have not pursued my dream career because I am afraid I do not have enough education.

Negative:
I'm afraid to try because I think I will fail.

Counteract:
I can do anything and can succeed at it because I really want it, and I will give my best.

Positive A: You are brimming with potential.

Do not let fear stop you. Do not be afraid to pursue your dream.

Education is not confined to a classroom. Education comes from various sources; experience, books you can read at your own leisure, the internet, etc. Who says you can't live your dream? Do the research. If it is your passion, pursue it relentlessly. Find out what you need to do. Don't get discouraged if you cannot work your desired career at this moment. Set a plan. Find out if there are alternate jobs that are similar. Really pinpoint what you love doing. Are you a good cook or baker? Perhaps you'd like to do some catering. Do you love to teach? Volunteer for Sunday School or substitute in your local school. Look for any opportunity that will hone in your skills and develop them. Remember practice makes perfect. Also, you have potential to do anything you dream!

Positive Actions will always shut down
fearful and negative dialogues,
and will push you through the doors of opportunity.

Emotion:

I am a bit shy and I am afraid to share my thoughts in any group setting. I know that I can contribute positively, and even find myself arguing certain points inside my head.

Negative:

I am afraid of making a fool out of myself by saying something stupid.

Counteract:

I believe in myself. I am an intelligent individual. I owe it to myself to shine.

Positive A: Your opinions and thoughts are important.

Do not let fear keep you silent.

Think about what is the worst thing that can happen if you say something that brings a rebuttal, or that is against your beliefs? It will bother you, naturally. How you react is what is important. You can defend your stance or listen to the difference of opinion and weigh it against your own. You can take it or leave it, however, learn not to take it personal. All of us have our own views. That is the beauty of this whole mish-mash world we live in. Start with baby steps. Speak up first with your closest friend(s). Join FB and post your thoughts and comment on other's posts. It'll help you build your confidence. Self-belief will boost your inner-view and help you to be comfortable with yourself and others.

Positive Actions will always shut down
fearful feelings and dialogues,
and will <u>give you the courage to be your "real" self</u>.

Situation:
I keep meeting and dating the wrong type of guys. I'm afraid I won't find Mr. Right. The last guy left me.

Negative: What's wrong with me?

Counteract:
My value as a person is not based on or defined by any person outside of me. (Most of us would be tempted to scream, 'his loss' and that may not be an entirely bad idea. What we are really trying to communicate and what your internal dialogue should be is: "His leaving and past failures are not indicators of *your* self-worth.")

Positive A: You are strong and valuable.

Do not let fear keep you at a vulnerable disadvantage.

Instead of jumping into another relationship, take this time as an opportunity to focus on you. This will be a good time to step back and build *you* up. Perhaps you're being over-analytical and like to dissect the reasons why, or maybe the whys overwhelm you. In either case, be kind to yourself. None of us can force someone to love us. Take this time to do all those fun things you didn't have time for. Surround yourself with a positive and uplifting support. Forgive the offender(s) and yourself, if need be. It will free you. Remember, you are strong and valuable just as you are—with or without a relationship in your life.

Positive Actions will shut down
fearful feelings and dialogues,
and will teach you
the importance of self-kindness and inner healing.

How do you get out of the grip of fear? First, you must assess what types of fears you've experienced; the healthy (hot stove) kind or the "I'm behind invisible-bars" type of fear. If you've answered yes to the second one, the next step is to stop running, and to step up and face your fear. Ask yourself, what caused this fear? Are your feelings legit or have they been blown out of proportion?

Once you answer those questions honestly, you can begin to set yourself free. One of the ways you can move on is to forgive. Yes, forgive. Why is it important to forgive? Fear is fueled by unresolved anger and hurts. You cannot move forward until you make the decision to let the hurt and anger go. Forgiveness isn't passive, it requires action. The first step is to say it. Be it to yourself or to the person who offended you. This is the first step towards wholeness. Once said, even if you don't feel it, forgiveness begins the process of freedom. A lot of times you won't feel like forgiving. However, once you take the first step, total forgiveness will eventually follow.

Forgiveness frees you from hurts. When you don't forgive, fear continues to hold you through anger, guilt and resentment. The job of these three emotions combined is to suck the life and joy right out of you. When you let these negative emotions go, you will feel liberated and empowered. Often times, you can be harsh and not forgive, or feel you don't deserve to be forgiven. The act of forgiveness is not a sign of weakness but of strength. The hardest thing to do is to forgive yourself. However, once you do, it allows you to live, really live, free and whole. As long as you choose to harbor negative emotions, you will remain a shadow of your true self.

What will you choose today?

No More Inward Run Assignment

You run inward when you don't face your fears and that includes the forgiveness of others and of self. It's important to shine and show off the confident you.

- List the areas where there is an inward run inside of you.
- Ask what is the worst thing that can happen if you stopped and faced each uncomfortable situation? Be realistic. What is the best thing that can happen? Be realistic.

Face it.
Acknowledge it.
Plan how you're going to get past your fears.
It may require forgiving yourself. Get past the guilt.
It may require forgiving someone else.
It may require changing your internal dialogue. (See chapter 1.)
It may require you to take a risk (that is not hurtful to you).
It may require change of your environment.
It may require change within a relationship(s).
It may require setting or changing your expectations to realistic ones.
It may require outside (positive and/or professional) help.

This list can go on, and on depending on the situation. Think of what positive action you can do to get past your fear. Then do it.

Make your motto…
No Fear, Just Courage…for all life's changes.

The Haunt
of
Constant
Doubt

Ghost of Insecurity

The haunt of insecurity causes questions of self-worth,
individual value, knowledge, appearance and potential.
These questions play in unison and form a chaotic noise
like an orchestra without a conductor.

The strongest are brought down to their knees, for the power
of insecurity has labeled them weak.

Yet life, in its kindness, brings those who see strength, not
weakness. It is the graceful few, who remind those who hurt,
that ghosts are transparent, and that courage is the journey past
all insecurities.

Insecurity Introduction

Have you ever had the jitters during the preparation to meet someone new, starting a new job, new school, new anything? We often question if we can accomplish what is set before us. We start to wonder if we look good enough, if we're talented enough, or if we got what it takes. Let's face it, no matter how confident we are, the feelings of insecurity washes over everyone at one time or another. The difference is, do we walk past those insecurities, or do we let them overpower us and let them dictate our living.

Have you ever heard of the disease called anemia? This illness affects millions of people each year. This blood disorder occurs when the body manufactures too little red blood cells. It can also appear when damaged red blood cells are not replaced fast enough. Why does that create a problem? Our red blood cells carry oxygen. Oxygen gives us energy. Anemic people suffer from a variety of symptoms ranging from extreme fatigue, weakness, confusion, even sadness and depression, amongst other things.

Insecurity, like the body's anemia, affects you not only physically, but also emotionally, mentally and spiritually. The symptoms are very similar. It drains you to the point of giving up. It deteriorates your resolve, makes you feel bewildered and trapped. Insecurity will ensure that you live miserably and deprived. Imagine these are only a few of the symptoms.

Although insecurity is part of life, living in constant doubt should not be. It is normal to feel unsure and uncertain when you are faced with certain challenges or new ventures. However, experiencing these emotions on a daily basis, under normal circumstances, is unhealthy and downright harmful.

Let's step back into the ladies' lives. Reading about their experiences may help you identify some areas in your life where the *Ghost of Insecurity* may have caused you to believe that you are inadequate or undesirable.

Insecurity Story

Dee decided to give Aggie a call the night she returned from her father's house. She wanted to thank her again for holding the luncheon.

"Hey Aggie, it's me Dee."

"Hey lady!" Aggie replied happily. "How are you? What's going on?"

"Everything is good. Hey before I forget, did Ellie leave already for vacation?"

"Yes my sweet cousin left to sunny Hawaii early this morning. She actually had a modeling shoot scheduled for early evening, before she officially starts vacation tomorrow."

"Lucky witch." They both said at the same time and chuckled.

Dee then began to recount the day's event. "Aggie, I tell you, it was liberating to finally feel like I fit in. **I thought I had failed when it came to my dad's expectations**. I wish I had spoken about it a lot earlier. I felt like I was an **outcast, an outsider**. You know what was weird, I knew it wasn't true, but I had so much **doubt in my heart and mind,** and that **clouded my reality**. I guess I was a lot like Leena. **I became skeptical and had constant distrust when it came to my own judgment**. Isn't that something?"

"Dee, I'm glad your dad helped you get past your insecurities. Although valid as they may have seemed because of what was going on in your life for the past few years, you should not let them ever define who you are. I always viewed you as a successful woman. As a matter of fact, I admire you. Woman, you juggle so much and you're raising a son by yourself. Give yourself some credit."

Dee's eyes began to water. "You know Aggie, thanks for the compliment." She resisted the urge to tack on a negative interjection. The knowledge that Aggie was a vice-president for a large division in a marketing firm started to make her feel **inferior**. However, she quickly reminded herself that her friend loved her, and that status comparison was irrelevant in their relationship.

"You're welcome honey. You know I read this real interesting article that hit the nail on the head. It's such a coincidence because it was about insecurity."

"Really?" Dee's interest peaked.

"Yes, the article was about abusive managers in the work place and how they hide their insecurities by misusing their authority. They wield their influence and control to cover their **lack of self-confidence**. They named the insecure manager Ms. Bin-security, short for Ms. Boss Insecurity."

"Ha ha, that's cute," Dee interjected wanting to hear more.

"Let me read you part of it. It was pretty interesting." Aggie sped off to get the magazine from her bedroom. Moments later she returned.

"Ok here it goes. Well, Ms. Bin-security was a very influential business woman in her industry and usually held a staff meeting once a day. It was her way of making sure that each of her projects was progressing as planned.

Ms. Bin-security started the meeting by saying, 'I've been monitoring the progress of the team and have observed the steady growth within our organization. Some may view me as a **control** freak but as you see my antics are working and I am proof of success. Remember, you are only as good as I make you, and keep in mind that without me, you are all nothing. Ladies and gentlemen I run this outfit.'

She looked straight across the room. All employees had an E (for employee) in front of their name. She wanted to make sure there was a clear distinction between her position and theirs."

"Oh gees," Dee rolled her eyes and smiled. Aggie continued

'E-Pretzel! Why are you so bent? Loser! You should straighten up that **posture**. I wouldn't want anyone to mistake you for her!'

She quickly turned to her right to E-Quiver, 'What in the world are you **afraid** of?'

Immediately to the right of E-Quiver was E-Whimper whose sniffles had become an annoying interruption. 'You still **don't trust anyone** here I see.'

As she studied the room her smile became wider, her eyes wild with growing satisfaction. Unexpectedly, her smile changed into a twisted snarl when she noticed E-Gloomy balled up in a corner.

'Hmmm, just where I want you; **depressed and alone**.'

She went around the table one by one, reviewed their progress, making sure she kept their flaws before them and apparent to all their peers.

Her eyes roamed to the last two at the table. E-Disgust looked at her with abhorring eyes. His **lack of love** and **self-acceptance** kept him in hurtful silence. Sometime ago he and E-Immature were an item, but Ms. Bin-security's persistence kept them apart. She convinced E-Immature that there was **no need for her to grow up**.

Her smile broadened even further, 'Ah' she sighed with contentment. 'What is the color of the sky in your world?' She didn't wait for a reply and continued, 'Meeting is adjourned. I see that you're all doing exactly what I want.' "

Aggie laughed and Dee chimed in, "Wow."

Insecurity Lesson

Dee had not only experienced fear but also insecurity. The difference between the two is that fear keeps you in your negative situation. Insecurity will sustain the growth of your negative emotions like a plant that needs water to sustain growth.

Do you think that Dee **felt inferior** compared to her siblings because of her lack of schooling and her job? Yet, Dee was blessed. Although she was **unsure of herself,** she had a dad who helped her see that it was a temporary perception that needed to be adjusted. A lot of people tend to **measure themselves based on their position** within their jobs, family, home, community, church, league, etc. They create a dependency on outside validation.

I like to imagine that Insecurity is a woman. Once she has a hold of you, she clings on to you for dear life, almost like a lover. Oh and be careful if you cross her because her grip will become vengeful. She will keep you in your place by instilling **fear** that is fueled with **doubt, or lack of love and trust**. It will show in your **posture** since she'll make sure you **lack the self-confidence and acceptance** that you need in order to succeed. Lady Insecurity will make sure you **hide your uncertainties** by keeping people at a safe distance. She wouldn't want any of them to get too close to you. People may find out about your **instability** and try to help you. Oh but wait. She has that covered too. You see, she'll also make sure that she stunts **your personal growth** by whispering that you're okay just the way you are. Her motto is, "Have problems? Don't face them." This will resound in your head like a lullaby. She'll love you forever and be your faithful friend as long as she's the Boss.

Wouldn't you agree that it may be time to fire her?
Many times, you are afraid to move forward because Lady

Insecurity keeps telling you that you're going to get hurt or fail again. The worst thing that you can do to yourself is to believe the lies that others have told you, or even worse the lies you say to yourself. You can become your own worst enemy. **Not only do you talk yourself out of something, but you talk yourself down, and crush your own self-esteem.** Aren't you happy to know that you now have the power to change that?

Let's look at a few examples and see how you can blow past your insecurities.

Situation:
Downsizing has caused me to get laid off. I don't believe I can get a job that pays as well because of my age.

Negative:
I doubt that there will be any jobs out there that I will qualify for.

Counteract:
I will find a job that will meet my needs and will make good use of my skills.

Positive A:
You are confident and capable.

It's important that you become proactive in your search.

You need to start to believe in yourself because if you don't, no one else will. Job hunting is basically marketing your abilities and skills. Write everything down that you know how to do. Your resume will never capture everything so be prepared to share all your strengths, skills and abilities. Consider what you like doing the most. You may discover you don't want to go back to corporate America and that perhaps it may be time for you to start your own business. In any case, turn over every possible stone of opportunity in the search process and don't give up. Remember, you are strong and capable of doing anything you desire. Believe in yourself.

Positive Actions will always shut down
doubt-filled, negative dialogues,
and will provide the certainty needed through any transition.

Emotion:
I don't date because I don't want to end up with somebody like my dad and get hurt like my mom did.

Negative:
I doubt I will have a successful relationship since my parents didn't.

Counteract:
My life will not be the same as my parents. I will have a good relationship with my future spouse.

Positive A: You deserve a great relationship.

Your past should not determine your present or your future.

There are many women today who had the wrong validation and affirmation by a male figure. However, in all of us there is common sense and a gut feeling that helps us determine right and wrong. The problem is that we settled for less. Don't settle any more. Aim high because you deserve to get and receive the best. Wait for the right person and learn to listen to yourself when the wrong guy comes into your life. The next time a good guy approaches you, take your time and get to know him. Write all the positives and negatives for you to see and weigh. Don't compromise when it comes to your happiness. In the meantime, enjoy who you are while you wait. Believe it or not, there are a lot of fish in the sea and it still has quite a few really good guys hidden amongst the losers you may have already encountered.

Positive Actions will always shut down
doubt-filled, negative dialogues
and will <u>affirm you when making relationship choices</u>.

Situation:
My family is big on fashion and fitness. I've always been the odd ball in size and dress.

Negative:
I doubt I will ever fit in with normal, beautiful people.

Counteract:
I fit in, not because of what I look like or because of my size, but because of who I am.

Positive A:
Your uniqueness is a gift.

The saddest thing that the media has done is to create robots in our generation.

If we don't dress a certain way or have certain lifestyles, we're not "in." We were not all made to be size 0-4. Society's norm has a way of reinforcing unhealthy attitudes towards our body. Life is not all about looks. The beauty of life is that God made each of us unique. We were meant to be diverse and singular. Don't ever feel like you need to apologize for being a size X. (X is by no means a large but anything above size 4!) All of us have special, lovely, and unique qualities. Write yours down and practice being content. Begin to count all of the blessings associated with what makes you special.

Positive Actions will always shut down
doubt-filled, negative dialogues
and will <u>show off your unique characteristics</u>.

Insecurity usually does not pop up overnight. A lot of times, it stems from something in the past that was reinforced over a long period of time. We usually don't identify a particular issue until the insecurity suffocates or stunts our emotional and spiritual growth.

During a time of soul-searching and evaluation, I had to face the reality of my own insecurities. Valid as they may have seemed at the time, one thing was for certain, in order for change to kick in, I had to change my pattern of thinking. This meant I had to build a staircase of faith and trust within myself.

The opposite of insecurity is confidence. You cannot have confidence in who you are, unless you start to believe and affirm that you are a trustworthy person. Often, you may gauge yourself by what you see. Don't wait to see to believe. Have faith. Faith is being certain in what you don't see.

Think about how special you are and what you can accomplish. Imagine all the things you can do. Visualize yourself as a confident woman who can achieve her dreams, no matter what challenges come her way. An affirmation is a declaration. In this case, the declaration is about the confidence in you. There should be a constant declaration in your mind of your trustworthiness that encourages you to build your staircase of confidence. The mind is like a sponge that constantly absorbs information. Make sure that your information is good and uplifting!

The key to change bad habits is the willingness to be flexible and teachable. For example, if a woman criticizes herself each time she looks in the mirror, she will eventually create and develop a low self-esteem. However, if this same woman praised herself daily about her positive attributes (and believe me, we all have them) her mind-set, or pattern of thinking will change.

Have you ever seen the demeanor of a confident woman? No

matter what her size is, she commands attention whenever she enters a room. What's stopping you from being that woman? It's time for you to peel off that insecure skin and let the confident you step out!

No More Insecurity Assignment

You become insecure when you believe that the negatives in your life define you. It's important to keep the positives before your eyes and in your ears to build and change your perception of self.

- List the areas where you may feel insecure.
- What positive action can you do to counteract each item on your list? Write down what you will do and make a commitment to stick with it.

What is the one dream or goal that you've not pursued because of fear and insecurity?

Life is too short to miss out on great opportunities. What insecurity has stopped you from living out your dream?

Go get that writing pad and put that dream on paper!!!

Are you excited? I am for you.

The Confident Woman is a Paradigm of Self-Love.

Discover
Wonderful
You

Something Better

It's better to say that it is, than it was.
It's better to say that it was, than it never shall be.
It takes less energy to aspire and achieve,
than to regret and fail.
For every endeavor in life, there's a price.
Be it small or big, it requires the investment of self.
The absolute ecstasy of life is living your dreams, and
knowing that there is still more to come over the horizon.

Wonderful You Introduction

Perhaps by now you feel like you've begun to steer your life in the right direction. Do you feel great? You've stepped up to the plate and have stopped living the life of pretense. You've mustered up the courage to face life's good and bad in this journey to become a self-assured, balanced, and healthy woman. Now let's tap into your unique qualities. It's time to embrace the excellent attributes that you already possess.

Did you know that you have a wealth of opportunities that dwells inside of you? Do you know that you hold the key to release all the goodness, power, and dreams that are locked inside your heart? I am sure that they have banged on the door to get out many times, but you were unable to hear them! Why? There was too much noise inside your head to hear it! Negative, self-talk, plays and replays inside your mind and drowns out the voices of good, and the affirmations and power that are within you.

Sometimes life beats us up so badly that we forget the good things and dwell on the negative. We become our own martyrs, slowly killing our self-esteem. When we hear the voice of a new opportunity, we view it as an opposition and our negative self-talk kicks into high gear. We shoot down our own dreams before they can even take flight. We contaminate our own soil of growth by our thoughts and how we speak to ourselves internally. No wonder there's so many of us that are stuck.

Let's visit with our ladies once again and see how Ellie's life is unfolding after her photo shoot and vacation.

Wonderful You Story

Ellie walked into her apartment exhausted. Her flight home had been delayed for five hours because of a snow storm. Although she had gone away to do a modeling shoot, the last half of her trip allowed her to island hop the six Hawaiian Islands. On the islands, she did a lot of soul searching. She also hoped she would come back recharged. Ellie felt anything but recharged as she dropped her luggage and flopped onto her couch.

As a model, her life revolved around glamour, yet, she had become increasingly unhappy with what she was currently doing. Ellie got her first big break when she was 14 years old, and decided early on not to pursue a formal education. Her high profile lifestyle and job afforded her many things, but she realized that even though her friends had less than her, they possessed one thing she didn't have…happiness. Her career wasn't all glamorous. It consisted of stressful schedules, hours of photo shoots, never-ending parties and no privacy.

With a sigh, Ellie grabbed her phone to listen to her messages. After a few moments, she put it down in disgust, then picked it up again and called her cousin.

"Hello," a sleepy voice on the other end answered.

"Hi Aggie, it's me Ellie. I'm sorry I woke you up but I really need to talk."

"It's okay, what's up, how was your trip?" Aggie was met with silence on the other end. "Ellie are you okay? What happened?" She heard only violent sobs. "Okay look I'm going to get dressed and come over and I'll be there in 30 minutes okay?"

"Okay," Ellie whispered and softly hung up the phone.

❧

Her world seemed to be caving in.

"**I'm no good**," she thought to herself. She repeated it over and over again, "**I'm no good**."

Ellie's thoughts were interrupted as she heard Aggie frantically calling out her name. She was grateful at that moment that she had given Ellie a key to her apartment.

❀

"Ellie, Ellie where are you?"

Aggie found Ellie curled up in a ball on the couch. Aggie dropped to her knees, threw her arms around Ellie and silently prayed, "God help me to help her." She asked out loud, "Ellie what's wrong honey, what's wrong?"

"I'm no good, I'm no good." The words tumbled out in an anguish cry.

Aggie rocked Ellie softly as she prayed for wisdom to help deal with whatever her cousin was going through.

Finally, Ellie's sobs subsided. She turned to Aggie, "Why couldn't I be like you?"

"Because you're not, besides why would you want to be me silly? I mean look at me…girlfriend you would want this?" She said pointing to her hips.

Ellie gave her a crooked smile. "Now that's my girl. Tell me what's going on."

Ellie wiped her face as more tears streamed down her cheeks.

"For years I have wanted to do something else besides modeling but all I kept hearing was 'All you have are your looks honey. You have no brains, sweetheart, forget it.' "

"Oh Ellie but that's a lie, hon. How can you believe that?"

Aggie held her cousin's face in her hands. "You don't believe those lies, right?"

Ellie's eyes began to swell with fresh tears. "You don't understand. **I've done things**," She stammered, "Things that…" The sobs began again.

Aggie wrapped her cousin in her arms and began to rock her softly again. She kissed her head. "No matter what it is you have done, how hurtful it has been to others or yourself, I'll always love you. I will always love you Ellie. Whatever it is, we can fix it together. I will be with you." She repeated this over and over again.

Ellie looked away in **shame**. "I did things to get certain jobs and to advance my career. **I am ashamed** of what I've done. **I don't feel good about who I am or what I have done. I've compromised my beliefs.** Gosh, if my mom or anybody in the family would find out, **I would be considered trash. I live with guilt. I feel worthless** and like **I can't accomplish anything,** because **I'm just not good.** Do you understand me? **Others would think less of me** if they found out, and the people I work with already think that way."

"I don't." She looked her cousin in the eyes and repeated, "I don't." She paused letting the words sink in. "Ellie none of us are perfect...none of us. **We all mess up from time to time...some of us worse than others.** The question is, now that you've gotten to this point, what do you want to do?"

"I have broken my contract and in doing so, I may be sued. I am giving up this apartment because a few people have the key. I know what you're thinking. You're wondering why I don't just change the lock. I don't want to. I just want to leave and start new. I was thinking of starting my own business."

"Oh really, what do you want to set up?"

Ellie's face finally lit up, "I want to start my own modeling agency, but unlike where I came from, I want to make it mandatory that every model enroll and complete a college education. I also plan to have a therapist on staff that will be responsible for doing evaluations before and after hire. You see, I don't want the girls to be exploited like I was. I want to teach them that looks aren't everything. I want them to know that they possess so much more inside. It's so important that they study, do what they love and not believe those who say they can't." Ellie's words tumbled out.

Aggie couldn't help but interrupt. "Do you hear yourself girlfriend? You keep saying there is nothing good about you and yet, you care enough to want to help others. Who more will these girls listen to than someone who has been there, done it and got burned. You lived the dream the wrong way, lived to tell it and care enough to warn them. And you say you have nothing good left inside of you?"

Ellie gave Aggie a defeated smirk that slowly turned into a smile.

"Ellie, it's time to stop looking at the bad, and focus on the good that is inside of you. I see it. I've always seen it, but now it's your turn to. No matter how much you've accomplished so far, you will never be able to reach the next level in life if you can't see 'your' good."

Wonderful You Lesson

So how do you get unstuck?

Let's review what has been done so far.

First, you had to remove the mask(s) that kept your hurts hidden. There is no fix until you identify and remove these masks. You probably discovered that in doing so, there were fears that started to choke you in the process, and one of the hardest steps was not to run, but face them.

Once you faced your fears, you were forced to acknowledge that they were fueled by some insecurity. You then, perhaps, discovered that constant doubt and insecurity kept you from reaching certain goals.

All of the exercises uncovered certain areas of your life that needed change. You were encouraged to acknowledge a variety of fine qualities and positive attributes about yourself to counteract the negative.

Did you know that you possess a well of potential that brims with possibilities? You have lots and lots of good stuff just waiting to gush out. However, it's not enough to just "know" the good about yourself. It needs to be drawn out of the well.

Have you ever felt overwhelmed with **guilt** or engulfed with that feeling of **I'll never amount to anything, I'm not good enough,** or **I'll never measure up.** Believe it or not, all of us have these feelings. Some of us have had these feelings due to years of verbal abuse. Others feel this way because of guilt over things done in the past. A number of us have these emotions because we are perfectionist, and we never measure up to our own perfect perceptions. These are just a few examples. There are many reasons why these negative emotions and self-talk invade our lives.

Have you ever wished that there was someone there for you during those times of utter despair? I know I do. It's such a blessing to have friends or family when you feel lost. Those special people help you see the good in you when your mind is completely clouded. How many times have you condemned yourself, even tortured yourself and have become the guilt-trip queen? There is a big difference between being remorseful and the constant beating up of you. Regret should go hand-in hand with change. Feeling regret or remorse over an action or event is only healthy when you move to a place of acknowledgment, responsibility, and forgiveness. The end result is that you move past it.

Perhaps our friend Ellie has reached that point. It's not uncommon for people to hit rock bottom or close to it before they take this very important action. When guilt is harbored and carried like a (false) medal of honor, it is a clear demonstration that you are in a crippled state of being. When '**I am less than, I don't deserve anything, and I'm not worthy**', becomes part of your voice and thought process, you maim and damage yourself emotionally, mentally, and spiritually. When you do not acknowledge the good inside of you, it paralyzes you from moving forward and upward. You cannot counteract anything negative unless you recognize, pull out, and keep in the forefront all the good stuff you possess inside.

Let's see how we can rip off those medals of (false) honors.

76

Situation:
All my life, people closest to me have told me that I will never amount to anything.

Negative:
Maybe they're right.

Counteract:
I refuse to believe in the lies of my past. I will begin to do what I have to do to change my current situation.

Positive A: You are persistent and have a can-do attitude.

Do you know that old saying, *if at first you don't succeed…try-try again?*

Failing in any area does not dictate or define who you are, or what your entire life is all about. Everyone fails at something in their lifetime. However, you have to choose how you react to the temporary failures. Failure should be viewed as an opportunity to learn and grow, not as a catastrophe. It is through the failing process where you learn to avoid certain pitfalls and find other ways to reach success. The next time you hear those negative voices filled with lies going on inside your head, yell the word STOP. Don't let them torment you anymore. Stop the noise and replace your mental tape with good and positive words! You are good and can do amazing things as a contributor in your life's journey.

Positive Actions will always shut down
lying voices and negative dialogues,
and will help you define the true you.

Situation:
My grandmother always told me that I'll end up with a bum like my mother did, because I am like my mom. I finally met someone I really like, but what if my grandmother is right?

Negative:
Why should I bother? It's true. I'm just like my mom.

Counteract:
I am my own person and deserve to be loved and happy.

Positive A: You are a loveable person.

People who love us often think that they protect us when, in actuality, they've hurt us with their words -- a lot of times without realizing it.

There comes a time in your life when you really need to stop, really weigh what has been said to you, and then make a decision on its validity. You are a unique individual. No matter how you were influenced, you will never be like any other person. The beauty of choice is that it redefines you constantly. Love is a wonderful experience. Don't let it slip by you because of your past or because of someone else's shallow view. Let go of other's history and make some of your own.

Positive Actions will always shut down
negative external voices and internal dialogues,
and will <u>open up the doors to receive love and happiness</u>.

Situation:
I have done things in my past that I'm not proud of. I have started over, but I don't think the people in my life are as forgiving as God.

Negative:
I'll always be what I was. Nothing will change.

Counteract:
I have changed and am determined to continue as the new me.

Positive A: You are a new person with a bright future.

Do you still walk with a curved posture and a downcast face?

If so, it's time to straighten up and hold that head up high. No one is perfect, and although some people are slower to forgive, the only person you need forgiveness from is God. As hurtful as it may be during the transition period because of the lack of acceptance, don't waiver and stand firm. Only God knows your changed heart and sees the true potential in your life. He knows that you possess a wealth of good and that you can do magnificent things. After all, He made you! It's your turn now to believe that, no matter what anybody may say or not say. This isn't about them. It's about you and your coming out into the world with a fresh new start. As you continue your journey, know that I applaud you for your courage and determination, and will be rooting for you in spirit.

*Positive Actions will always shut down
the past, negative dialogues
and will reveal the new you.*

Have you ever had one of those friends when every time you mentioned a negative thought, they'd make it a point to make you see the positive? After a while, it would probably annoy you to no end. I have one such friend. During many conversations, I found myself analyzing my thoughts before I spoke.

You have to get to the point where you realize that, no matter how bad things seem, there is always something to be grateful for. This gratitude, attitude-adjustment will help you understand that challenges have a purpose in your life. They make you grow and learn, and help you to become stronger and happier in the end. I don't know about you, but I sure like knowing that things are good and will get better. To dwell on the negative is never healthy. Notice I used the word dwell. It is normal to feel sad, blue, or even depressed at times, but it's not healthy to stay there.

Now repeat after me…
I am good.
I possess good.
I am grateful for all that is in my life.

Now say it again convincingly and don't ever forget it!

4

Wonderful You Assignment

You are reminded of wonderful when you become aware of all the good you possess. It's important to speak positive about yourself so that you can embrace unique you.

- List your good qualities. What are they?
- What positive action can you take to build any weak areas? Write down what you will do and make a commitment to stick with it.

List 3 affirmations that you will say over yourself every day when you get up each morning.

**The thought of something better,
propels you into destiny's path.**

The
Strength
To
Choose

Realm of Choice

Broken promises whether to ourselves or to others
always seem to take the shape of something unexpected,
when in reality, it was a choice we've made.
The hardest of choices
requires that a stance be taken during adversity
although we'd rather run or cower.
The easiest of choices
is when carelessness reigns in the heart
with the illusion that there is a future without limits,
promised and at our disposal.
The wisest of choices
looks at the horizon as a potential painting.

Your Choices Introduction

Ever been in a place where you felt that you had to do something because you had no other choice? Perhaps you felt trapped, or felt that the risk or pain was the driving factor for your resolution. Often, we fail to see that we have a realm filled with choices because the focus is on the discomfort that the situation causes.

Sometimes the past can blind us. We think that we are who we are and that history will continue to dictate and remain the same, but is that really true? Do we not possess the ability to forge our future and reshape our destiny?

Now that you have started to embrace the good that you possess, it's time to look at the choices you have made, will make today, and will make in the future. You have already made one valuable choice. You have decided to invest time into yourself by reading this book. You love yourself enough to want to make the necessary changes to grow.

Your life's growth process is a choice. You can decide to be idle or you can make the decision to move forward even when it means you have to wait for certain things to come to pass. To move forward means that you do what is necessary to reach your goals even if it takes time to achieve them. It is important to remain persistent whether you are waiting for change inside, or waiting for circumstances to change around you. For example, if you want to become an artist, you must practice your craft to master it. It may require going to school or getting an instructor. How do you keep your vision to become an artist strong and in your sight? Start to collect positive quotes and affirmations that will help you shape your vision. Get examples or pictures of art pieces, blurbs of stories and struggles of famous artists. This shapes the correct expectations inside and outside of you. In the wait to become great, you contribute and invest in your talent and in your self-value.

Ellie found the secret to making choices. She stopped thinking *entirely* with her heart and emotions, and started to think and weigh with her head and her logic.

Let's look at how her new attitude unfolds, and how Leena and Dee's choices changed their lives.

Your Choices Story

Everyone was happy to get together once again so soon. This time, they all met at Ellie's house to help pack for the move. Aggie looked at Leena who was stretched halfway across the sofa with her feet up on the ottoman. She had a peaceful look. It resembled the same look that Ellie and Dee had. She knew it was because of the choices each of them had recently made. All had **decided to face their fears and issues**, and all had **opted to make life better**.

"Okay you've been staring at me for a while. What are you smiling about?" Leena sassed.

Aggie smiled and happily answered "I can't help but be happy for the three of you. I mean look at you. You have a different aura about you. You guys now walk around with your heads held up high. You walk confidently, and exude a peaceful resolve."

"Oh gosh she's getting therapeutic on us!" Ellie dripped sarcastically.

Happy laughter echoed in the room. Leena left the room and returned with a tray.

"Okay, here ya go." Leena passed out cups of coffee, moved Ellie's legs and plopped down beside her.

Ellie caressed her arm softly. "So how are things going at home?"

"It's okay I guess for now. You know this was the hardest thing for me to do but **I decided it was time to stand up for myself and not allow him to hurt me anymore**."

"What exactly did you say or do?" Ellie pushed.

"I was afraid and did not want to talk to him by myself, because I wasn't sure how he was going to react. So **I asked** a pastor to set up a meeting with us both, and then I asked my brother to wait for me outside of the office, just in case things really blew up. I have to tell you, I was scared to death. I was shaking all the way to the pastor's office. Pastor and I purposely scheduled it on a week day so that I didn't have to drive in with him. Once I walked into that office, though, **I was determined** to tell him exactly how I felt, and what his neglect and constant need for control was doing to me. The session was brutal."

"I can imagine." Aggie nodded for her to continue. All eyes were fixed on Leena.

"He agreed to go to a therapist and has been going every single week. **I have learned** through our sessions that my techniques for compromise were all wrong. I was constantly doing it at my expense. There was no happy medium. Our negotiations were based on his decisions, and I let him. **I made the choice to let him have his way all the time, just to keep the peace**. I finally understood that **I let him take away my power** to say no or voice a contrary opinion. No matter how scared I am, or was, **I still possessed the control to alter the situation I was in**."

"We're very proud of you," said Ellie.

Leena quickly replied "What? Are you kidding me? We should be the ones that are proud of you. You're letting go of so much without the guarantee of recuperating half of this, all because you're doing what is right. It takes guts to do what's right some times."

"I guess we should all be proud of each other," Dee emerged from her silence. All eyes turned to Dee.

"The quiet one has spoken," Ellie broke in chidingly.

Like a rushing waterfall, Dee began to recount her story, and her decisions for change. Everyone listened in awestruck silence. Dee paused for a moment.

"Go on," Aggie encouraged her.

"**I decided I wanted to change my perception of me** inside. I always felt like I wasn't good enough. **I had to stop downplaying myself** in my head. **It took a bit of persistence and constant reminders,** but after a while, it became easier to make changes. Soooo, after much research, I've applied for a loan and have put a bid in for a hair place of my own down in Elmont."

"Woo-hoo," Ellie bellowed. "Group hug everybody. Our Dee is growing up!"

Once the laughter settled down, Dee put her hand on Ellie's shoulder.

"You know in the past that would have hurt me and I would have felt offended, and I would have left here without saying a word. However, today, I know you're saying that jokingly because I finally understand that you believe in me. I guess you were all waiting for me to believe in myself."

Aggie turned Dee around.

"We had to wait for **you to make the choice to better your life**. We knew you were very good at styling hair and could run your own place without a problem, but you needed to discover that."

"Yea, but it took me so long to get to this point. I've lost so much time."

"You know Dee, sometimes I feel like that -- like I've lost so much time. But **I've decided not to let the past hold me down** and **I'm determined to make the rest of my life my adventure**, nobody else's."

Ellie's eyes started to fill with tears as she continued. "I think the worst thing anyone can do -- a woman can do -- is to compromise herself in any way that is going to degrade or hurt her. There is no reason why a woman should sacrifice herself by using her body or anything else to get something. I think a lot of **women choose to forget** their value. They lower their standards and view themselves as less than. I have to say I didn't understand it until quite recently. **I made the choice to believe the lies**. I felt I needed to do what everybody else was doing to climb up to the top in my industry. Truth is, not everybody does that. I just felt it was right although I knew it was the wrong thing to do. **My decisions hurt me** and will probably hurt me for a long time."

Aggie put her arm around her cousin and pulled her softly towards her.

"The one thing that **helped me make the decision** to get out and start something new was your support. I was so wrapped up in my fast-paced world that I couldn't see that I could do better for myself. I couldn't get to that point until **I accepted that I was worth it**."

Your Choices Lesson

We should strive to live, work, and do what we love in excellence. Frequently, we get intimidated by the words *great* and *excellent* because we feel that we are undeserving and cannot carry those titles. We feel that we are okay. However, we fail to see that excellence should always be our goal. It doesn't mean we are conceited or want to be higher than anyone else. Your motivation should always be to live your best in all aspects and on every level. When you make the choice to see yourself through the eyes of greatness, it changes your perception. You begin to make your choices based on positives and truths, and not on negatives and lies. Ellie took the stance not to believe the lies of her past or the history she had written. She decided it was time to change her destiny even though she would lose a lot of what she presently had or owned.

The evidence of good choices is peace. It is not based on what feels nice but on what's right. Sometimes what's right may feel uncomfortable and it may hurt or even be devastating, especially when it requires you to let go of deep embedded lies. Know that the discomfort is temporary and is followed by tranquility. We have become a society with the mind-set of, *if it feels good, than its right*. Things that feel good, yet are not good, will eventually come back to bite you or worse, haunt you. The reason we get ourselves into these predicaments is because few of us like to wait. We want it now. It's called instant gratification. The other reason is because we'd rather compromise our values or our beliefs just so we can get what we want. When??? Now!

No one can take away your power to choose. They can intimidate you to the point of paralyzing fear, but it is your decision whether you allow them to continue. Repeatedly, fear will convince you that there is no other alternative. Fear forces you to stay stuck and imprisoned in situations you should either get out of or discontinue. Choices will always require action. Those actions start inside your mind in your way of thinking.

After Leena thought about it, she sought help for every area of her life. For example, Leena sought counseling from a clergy and her brother's protection. She did not do it alone. She understood that in order to break the vicious cycle in her marriage, she needed outside assistance and intervention. Leena's action included the decision to stop and say "enough;" the determination to change her situation; the plan for resolution (counseling); and the acceptance of the mistakes she made that contributed to the problem. You may be thinking, those are tough and uncomfortable steps, and you're absolutely right. However, the alternative is to stay exactly where you're at today.

Choices can make or break you. They can result in blessings or consequences. Even when you decide to change things for the better, your past decisions can have a ripple effect for a very long time. But, don't be discouraged. No, you cannot undo the past, but you can begin to shape your future by weighing all of your choices going forward. Don't beat yourself up and feel like you've wasted or lost time. You can't recuperate it, but you can decide today to break out of your comfort zone.

Start to dream again. Put it on paper if you haven't done so in the past exercises. Dream big! Don't be afraid if it seems impossible at the moment. Can you imagine how the guys who first dreamed up the space shuttle felt like? Yet, in time, it all came together and they achieved their ultimate goal. Time is never entirely lost when you decide to move into your purpose, into what you love.

Ellie uncovered another secret. She accepted the value of her worth. She had the choice to accept or reject that view of herself. This insight could not be revealed to her until she started to think differently. It required her to tweak her thought process. People don't change because they can't. They don't modify certain behaviors because they don't want to. Change, for the most part, puts one in an uncomfortable place.

We are creatures of habit. Habit equates to comfort after a while. Break that comfort. Create new habits. The wonderful thing about habits is that they can be broken. Replace the bad habits with good ones. This is what we've been doing all along.

Now the next step is to break out of the habit of bad choices, and replace those patterns with good ones. Let's look at a few examples.

Situation:
It's Christmas and you have experienced some financial hardships during the year. Most of your credit cards are maxed out.

Negative:
I'm already knee deep in debt. It doesn't matter if I use what's left on my open credit cards.

Counteract:
I will choose to review my budget and see what I can afford.

Positive A: You can manage your finances wisely.

Sometimes you just can't buy everyone a gift.

It's up to you to take responsibility and ownership of your debt. It doesn't belong to anyone else. It belongs to you, which means you can control it. You can proactively manage it when you cut down on your spending, or decide not to spend on things you don't need. You should not continue to please others at the expense of yourself. Financial hardship can hit any of us at any time because of job loss or illness or other reasons. Every now and then, you have to make decisions that will help you even if it means that others cannot or will not understand. Spend less, save more, and free yourself by bringing down and eliminating your debt. Why? It will eliminate a lot of unnecessary stress because you won't have to worry about paying for what you cannot afford. Make a choice to live within your means.

Positive Actions will always shut down
bad financial choices
and will help protect your assets.

Situation:
It is hard for me to establish an intimate relationship because I was abused.

Negative:
No one is ever going to want me because I'm damaged beyond repair.

Counteract:
I choose to acknowledge that it was not my fault, but I'm going to get help so I can feel better about myself.

Positive A: Your value is greater than the largest diamond.

The hardest thing a woman can go through is the experience of being violated. It makes her believe that her self-worth has been taken or stolen from her, especially if the harm done to her was over a period of time. Although she can't change the past, she can make a decision and alter her future. When a woman is hurt in this manner, it can imprison her to the point of making the rest of her life a miserable journey. However, if this is one of your experiences, you have the power to turn it around. Make the choice to take ownership of your future. Seek help and speak to a professional who can give you the tools to cope and change how you think. If you're still in the situation, seek help and get out. If you are a woman with an abusive past, I pray God's comfort over your life, and restoration for your soul, mind, and body. You are so valuable. Don't ever let anyone else tell you otherwise.

Positive Actions will always shut down
negative views of yourself and internal dialogues,
and will <u>reaffirm your value</u>.

Situation:
My marriage has been bad for a while, and there is a person I know who makes me feel wonderful.

Negative:
I want to be happy again and deserve it, even if it means it's with someone else.

Counteract:
I choose to weigh questions like: What can I do to fix my marriage? How did I contribute to the problem?

Positive A: You deserve love that is not hidden.

It is so easy to justify a wrong action if it's going to bring you happiness. Perhaps it will bring some joy to your heart and will even ease the pain, but it will not fix or remove the problem.

A marriage doesn't go bad because one person is doing something wrong. It goes bad because both parties contributed to it and that means you have ownership too. Instead of finding an outside release, take responsibility for your role within the marriage.

Get out of your comfort zone and admit there is a problem, do something about it. Tell your spouse that you're not happy and the reasons why, then take it a step further and seek help like counseling. If you are in an abusive relationship, get out, but don't forgo getting counseling for yourself anyway. Whenever you're tempted to go down that path, remember one thing, temporary fixes that are wrong will always hurt you, as well as those you love.

Positive Actions will always shut down
decisions that will hurt your heart,
and will a maintain healthy ownership balance.

What you choose today can either hurt or prosper your tomorrow. This is probably one of the hardest chapters. To take ownership of our choices stings at times, and when you admit that you haven't taken ownership, it can feel like putting salt in the wound. You are not alone. Many have chosen to ignore certain areas in their lives because they are just too painful or are a nuisance. Issues that are ignored will not go away until they are dealt with.

The flip side of choice is not being able to move forward. You cannot forge ahead until you accept that you have the ability to contribute towards your destiny.

We are all here for a unique purpose, however, it's each person's responsibility to discover it, and then live it. How do you want to continue living? Make it a point to turn things around. You can. I believe that you can. Why do I believe although I do not know you (yet)? I was you some years ago. I experienced the stepping up-to-the-plate for change, but I also knew the importance of taking ownership and responsibility for me. I cannot control anyone else's actions, but I sure have power on how I will react, and whether or not I will allow anything to continue.

Do you want to live life to the fullest? I know you do. Become courageous, or do it afraid, but don't stop…do it!

Your Choices Assignment

You will be presented with choices for the rest of your life. The good news is that you can choose wisely and start now. It's important to make good choices because you are worth it!

- List some of the major good and bad choices you have made.
- What positive action can you take to turn around a bad situation because of a bad choice? Write down your plan and stick with it.

Create a new good choice and habit that will benefit you. Start with something simple like 15 minutes of quiet time every day.

Exercise your power to choose.

**Did you know that the way you think is a choice?
The way you perceive yourself is a choice.**

The
Upside
of
Friendship

Precious Friends

The most precious of friends
come by rarely in a lifetime
They're gems that gain in luster
With each passing moment
Yes, a celebration of souls
an acclimation of unity
One of the warmest expressions
of Love

Friendship Introduction

I believe - with my entire heart - that friends are a precious and a necessary part of life. I understand the value of particular friendships that remain throughout life, and even those that are for a season. Intimate relationships can be the most rewarding or detrimental influence in our lives. Your choices can be deterred by those closest to you; by those in your inner circle.

Look back in your life. How often have your friends or family talked you out of something that perhaps was going to benefit you? How regularly have you been told that you cannot do something?

Now that you have your inside voice on the right track, the next step is to choose which voices you will allow or accept to speak into your life, going forward.

Friendship Story

Dee's heart hit the floor. Her mind went numb. She couldn't think or move. The doctor's words "three months" echoed in her mind. Her feet felt like they were glued to the floor. She saw people walk by her in slow motion going about their business. She felt her world caving in around her. It felt like an eternity before she could breathe again. "This can't be happening to me. It's too soon. He's too young."

She fumbled through her purse. Her cell phone had no service inside, and she didn't want to leave him alone in the room for too long. Dee needed to talk to somebody. Once outside, her fingers were clumsy and she entered the wrong numbers. She groaned and tried again. All she could get out was a sob when she heard the voice on the other end.

Leena began to panic. She didn't know at first which of the gals was on the line but after a few moments was able to figure out that it was Dee. Leena's heart began to pound hard in her chest. Her mind began to race as she started to brace herself for the bad news she was about to receive.

"Dee honey, it's okay, whatever it is, it'll be okay. Just calm down and tell me what's wrong, honey…talk to me. What happened?"

The sobs on the other end of the phone continued for what felt like an eternity. Leena kept reassuring Dee as she patiently waited.

Dee was finally able to quiet herself down and began in a rasping, painful whisper. "It's daddy, Leena; he has cancer."

"Where are you? What hospital?"

After giving Leena the information, she slid to the floor with her hand over her eyes. "God, how am I going to tell him? This is so unfair. He's only 62 years old. Oh my God, how am I going to tell him?"

She didn't want the doctors to break the news to him. She felt they would have been too cold and lacked compassion with their matter-of-fact tones. As she sat on the floor, she began to realize that the burden of breaking this type of news may have been better with the doctor. She was alone in the hospital. Dee had brought her father early in the morning to the emergency room because he had troubled breathing. Her brother was out of the country and she hadn't called her sister yet. Dee had lost her mother when she was very young and her father had tried his best to compensate. He never remarried after her mother's death.

She picked herself up slowly, grabbed her cell once again and called her sister. After the call, she walked towards the room where her father was waiting. As she opened the door, she knew life would never be the same.

❖

Leena called Ellie and Aggie. She told them not to go to the hospital just yet as she was heading down there to get more information and to support Dee. As she drove to the hospital, Leena began to imagine how Dee felt and tears began to well up in her own eyes. "I have to be strong for Dee. I need to focus and be strong for Dee," she said to herself.

Traffic was backed up and Leena started to get anxious. She knew she couldn't contact Dee at the hospital because her father was still in the ER.

❖

Rachel, Dee's sister, walked into the hospital, annoyed that she had to leave work early. Dee had called and relayed it was important that she come because her father was ill. It had been three years since she had seen her father. Her rise in the corporate world surrounded her with a lifestyle that included influential friends and colleagues whose main interest was to impress and supersede. The competition to maintain status within her field was fierce. Her family all but disappeared and her friends became her new family. Their opinions and views were what mattered most to her.

She inquired at the desk and was told what room he was in.

❖

Leena reached the hospital about 30 minutes after she hung up with Dee. When she entered the room, she wondered if she could keep her composure.

Herman smiled widely when he saw Leena at the doorway. "Come in, come in. Why do you look so pale? I'm okay. Come here." He scrunched up his nose in an exaggerative smelling gesture towards the bag. "Is that what I think it is?"

Leena had brought a bowl of chicken soup from the Spanish restaurant near her home. She knew how much Dee's father loved their soup. Leena glanced around and saw Dee and her sister,

Rachel, standing in the back of the room.

"Yes it is," Leena smiled widely as she began to set up his small feast.

Rachel's lips tightened as she turned steely to Dee. "Can I see you outside?"

❀

Rachel led Dee into the parking lot. She turned around and exploded, "How can you let people who are not considered family come to the hospital to feed our father when you should be doing that?"

Dee did not allow her to go on. "Who do you think you're speaking to? I am not one of the people in your office and I do not care if you're my older sister! Where have you been for the past three years? Not here! Leena is more his daughter than you have been. When was the last time you picked up the phone to call and find out how he was doing?"

Rachel's jaw dropped in disbelief. Her quiet sister had become a tigress. Before Rachel could get in another word, Dee looked her square in the eyes and continued to say what was on her mind. Dee's tone became calm and controlled.

Rachel remained quiet. Sadly, everything she heard was true. Finally, Rachel used the excuse that she had to get back to the office as an escape.

Before Rachel could get away, Dee hugged her and said, "I'm sorry if I was hard on you. I love you, I always will, but you're missing out on the most important part of your life…family."

Friendship Lesson

Friendship is an investment. The more connected you are, the greater trust there is and the returns can never be measured. During times of crisis, you will notice two things and the response you receive will determine the depth and longevity of the relationship.

An emergency will either 1. push someone away or 2. will draw them nearer. Not everyone is cut out to be supportive during a tragedy, illness or death. However, there are some people that will come into your life that not only stand by you, but will also hold you up during the storms. Everyone should have a core circle of these types of friends. Sometimes it includes family like a sister, cousin or aunt. I'm an advocate of friendship within family first. I'll talk more about that later.

Why is it so important that you have friends that you can depend on during crisis? Each of us will experience emergencies. We are not loners by nature. We grow personally when we have others that we can depend on from time to time. This type of support system is a good thing. Once in a while, we get hung up on taking care of ourselves, and that is not entirely a bad thing. However, when the care of self, pushes away those that can help you, it ushers in isolation, which in essence, puts you back in your cell. Aren't you tired of being in your little prison?

In the past, Dee would shut out her friends in her times of need because she felt that they wouldn't understand, and because she didn't like being vulnerable before them. She felt insecure and thought that they were better than her. Once she stopped the comparison and focused on her qualities, potential, and abilities, she was able to appreciate the deep friendships that she had forged over the years with Leena, Ellie and Aggie.

Notice, Dee had to fix her internal view first, before she could understand the value of her friendships. This helped her get to the point of trust and that in turn, brought comfort. The comfort produced security within her when her crisis arrived in her life. Even when she couldn't think straight, she knew that it was safe to call Leena. Dee knew in her heart that Leena loved her and would provide the support that she needed during this particular storm.

It may have seemed strange to you at first that Dee chose to call Leena first before her sister. Unfortunately, sometimes that is the reality of life. I have been blessed with an incredible sister. However, some of you either don't have a sister, or have one that you cannot count on.

What did you notice about Dee's sister? She had forgotten the value of family. Although this chapter focuses on friendships, it doesn't necessarily mean that those relationships should begin outside of the family unit. Friendships start at home. When your parents fell in love it was because either they were the best of friends or because they became the best of friends (in most cases).

The family should be the foundation, the example, of how to create outside friendships. Family should be a place of safety first and foremost. They should always be your first ally. Unfortunately, over the years some rifts are often created and are hardly ever repaired. Since family members know each other well, it's easier to keep grudges and to sling the past into each other's faces. But, what does that prove? What positive does that bring? It can never usher in the chance to heal. There is also the fact that some family members refuse the opportunity to heal. In that case, you have to know when to let go.

What is the beauty of good friendships? It always gives back to you and that giving usually spills over to those you love. Friendships become precious when they become part of your family. These people are the ones you tell your kids to call aunt or uncle. They are the people that will go above and beyond for you. It doesn't mean that they are necessarily present physically all the time. Sometimes it's just impossible. However, they do make it a point to be there for you in spirit and are constant and consistent in your life. These include the ones that live miles away, but can be counted on. You can call them at any time, no matter what.

Now let's look at what doesn't make a good friendship. One thing that is not part of camaraderie is jealousy. The moment you become envious, it causes you to compare. What comparison does is that it makes you feel inferior, even if you're smarter, wealthier, prettier, etc. Friendships dissolve because of this. All of the sudden someone that you thought was a good friend may turn on you, because you've found the man of your dreams, a new friend, a great job, gone back to school, etc. They begin to feel like they no longer measure up and become critical. Instead of encouragement, they'll continuously find fault with what you're doing, discourage you from following your dreams, and will even dig up your past secrets and use them against you. This pattern becomes hurtful and has a negative influence. You may even love your friends so much that you would rather give up what you have obtained then lose them.

What is the right price of your love tag? Love will never selfishly take away from you. If anything it will always add to you, in any relationship. Love will understand. Love will accept. Love will support. This means that your friend, a true friend, should be someone who accepts you for who you are, but is not afraid to tell you the truth, even when it hurts.

How many times have you compromised your beliefs, views, moral standing and dreams because of the love tag? You probably even heard it from others -- "but she's my friend, she loves me." Does she really?

A true friend will never come against you and intentionally hurt you. A real friend will tell you the truth because they care about you. You may not want to talk with them for a while, but deep down in your heart, you know they're right. I'm not talking about negative lies that tear you down. I'm talking about constructive criticism that is for your benefit and will help you grow. That is the big difference.

When friendship only benefits one side of the equation, it is not true companionship. Relationships require a healthy balance of give and take.

Let's review the following samples.

Situation:
My girlfriend is with someone that does not treat her right. When I told her how I felt, it created a rift between us. We are not on speaking terms.

Negative:
I would never put up with what she does. I'm not going to talk to her until she comes to her senses.

Counteract:
Wrong or right, is my motivation and delivery correct?

Positive A: You can speak your heart.

Notice we are not addressing your friend's situation but the focus is you.

What was your motive when you spoke to her? Did a past hurt trigger painful memories inside? Are your concerns valid or are they based on hearsay or one observation? How was your delivery?

In order to maintain good friendships, you have to be a good friend. Once you've checked your motives and have the facts, not what you feel, revisit and weigh it.

If it burdens you because it is detrimental to your friend, look again at your delivery. A person is more receptive when they're told in love and that sometimes means you ask for forgiveness first, especially if you've been quarreling.

Keep in mind that some people will not receive what is being said to them. Prepare yourself for that.

Remember you cannot control anyone, only yourself. If the friendship continues to be a negative impact to you, set a time-out period for the relationship. Time will determine if the friendship was only for a season.

Positive Actions will always shut down
questionable motives,
and will <u>help protect your emotional investment of self</u>.

Situation:
A co-worker, who I thought was a good friend, used all of my strategies as her own and was promoted because of it.

Negative:
I will never forgive her and will make sure she pays for it, even if it takes the rest of my life.

Counteract:
I will not stoop down to her level. My value is not determined by my job.

Positive A: You can manage your reactions.

I can hear some of you right now. "What, are you kidding me?!"

The initial reaction for most would be to go over to the co-worker and use a few choice words and perhaps become physical. The truth is that it would probably feel good for the moment, but it would not fix the problem in the long run.

Step back and look at the history of that friendship.

How much give and take was there?

Were you the giver most of the time?

What caused you to trust her enough to share anything that was important to you?

Was she the type that constantly asked for help and you as a good friend, bailed her out time after time?
Sometimes people take advantage of us, and it happens only

because we allow them to. We become blind and do not weigh whether the so-called friendship should be continued or if it should be changed to an acquaintance level.

If you are experiencing, or have experienced something like this, revenge is never the answer. Time has a way of taking care of these wrongs. In this case, someone up in management will eventually recognize where the knowledge really resides.

Positive Actions will always shut down
negative-attacks
and will maintain choices and balances in friendships.

Situation:
My friend flirts with my partner a bit too much and it makes me feel uncomfortable. When I tell her I don't like it, she dismisses it.

Negative:
I'm going to back off and not tell her anything anymore. Maybe, I'm just being jealous.

Counteract:
I am a good friend to her and expect the same from her.

Positive A: You have the ability to manage your boundaries.

Ask yourself this question first.
Are you the jealous type? (Be very honest with yourself.)

Is this the first time that this has happened to you or is your discomfort happening more often than not? If this feeling has happened once before, it may be that you're still dealing with some insecurity. Get to the root of that insecurity and fix it. Don't let it pass because it will haunt you, and it will rear up its ugly head again and again.

However, if this is the first time, ask yourself the following questions.

Why is this really bothering me?

Is it really disrespectful?

Has my partner encouraged this behavior?
Once you review the answers to these questions, determine who you will address and how you will do it. Remember delivery is very

important.

Bottom line is that someone who loves you and is a good friend, be it your partner or the offender-girlfriend, should respect certain boundaries, and will never create or put you in a position where you feel uncomfortable.

Positive Actions will always define
good boundaries,
and will <u>maintain respectful limits</u>.

Perhaps you have realized that friendship begins with you. You set the standard. Your return on your investment is dependent on who you choose and how much you put into the relationship. Basically if the return is not what you expect or want, you determine whether you want to continue. Like any relationship, it requires that both parties provide input to maintain a fine balance. You've learned that good friendships should promote growth and when embraced can often bring rewards like the connection with another's soul. Bad friendships will tear you down, and when you hold on to them will frequently cost you dearly.

Good and bad relationships can be seen inside and outside of the family structure. However, you have the power to choose which one you will continue in. Keep in mind that if you are in a position where a breakaway is required, it should be done wisely. You get nothing when you cut another person down or list their faults. Everyone has faults, including you.

There are situations where you may live with that someone and the last thing you need to do is to stir the pot. It's quite okay to voice your hurt but pick the right time and right delivery. For example instead of saying "YOU do this and YOU do that," try, "I would like to talk about certain things you brought up the other day. When you said this, did you mean that? Because, it made me feel like…" (Example:"The other day when you mentioned that I cannot be trusted. Can you give me an example of when I disappointed you? Those words hurt me because I could not recall when I betrayed you.") It takes away the focus from them and changes the focus to your hurt; how certain things made you feel. Word of caution, if the hurt runs deep you may want someone else to be there with you as a neutral party.

The choice to continue any friendship ultimately is yours. Some can be repaired and some are not meant to be.

In all accounts, true friendships should not be taken lightly. Each one of them is a gem in their own right.

Friendship Assignment

You deserve good friends and are capable of being a good friend. It's important to establish boundaries and to differentiate who will take away or benefit you as a person and who is able to give and receive friendship.

- List your closest friends. Who are they?
- Perhaps you are regretting that you allowed certain friendships into your life. Take that regret and throw it away. Purpose in your heart to take it as a lesson learned.
- What positive actions can you take to ensure that you do not make the wrong friendship choices going forward? Write them down.

Have you been a good friend to all or is there someone you lost touch with or perhaps you need to ask for forgiveness? Only invest your time and energy in the good friendships. Cut off all those friendships that are hurting you.

**Make it your heart's goal to surround yourself
with friends that will build you.**

Your

Heart

Matters

One Who Knows

From the depths of my heart springs forth life
a growth that exceeds comprehension
and yet recognized by those
who've walked the same path
reached the same abyss of sorrow
but who have climbed out into a world
of horizons filled with wondrous hues
that blend into a harmonious combination
of passion and fulfillment
Filling the future with wondrous expectations
A willingness to embrace
the beauty of acceptance of self and others
In this entangled journey
of uncertainty and unrelenting peace
that draws the soul to rest and final closure
the belief that propels us day-to-day
to be in wholeness, who we are
displaying the very essence
of One Who Knows

Your Heart Introduction

Throughout this journey, you've done a continuous evaluation of your life. Perhaps a few steps were very painful and difficult, especially when you had to be brutally honest with yourself. However, I'm sure you've done some changes that gave you positive results.

By now, you're probably feeling a bit lighter and freer than you've been feeling for a while. You've begun to create a better and peaceful you. As we continue together in this crossing to better living, there are a couple of things that you may still need to explore. Although you've identified and have worked on change, you cannot forget one of the most vital parts of your being -- your heart.

Your emotional repository should constantly flow into the lives of others. The condition of your heart determines whether you are a waterfall or a stagnant well. A heart that overflows with love, warmth, and gratitude can't help but pour the same into anyone who comes near. When you maintain an angry, icy, unappreciative heart, nothing can pour out of you and so your waters become motionless. Perhaps you're not in either extreme. Maybe you only experience those ill feelings for certain people because of certain memories. You've managed to create an on and off switch and have convinced yourself that you're in control. But, let me ask you, are you really in control?

When it comes to the matters of the heart, anything that takes residence will usually be the domineering force. Make no mistake, just because the resident lies dormant at times, doesn't mean it's not there. Sooner or later, it comes out and does its job. By the way, the resident will stop pestering you, when it is sure that your waters are once again motionless and stagnant. It hates change.

Your Heart Story

"Hey, what are you looking at?" Aggie put a finger towards her mouth, shushing Leena then pointed to the trees. Both were mesmerized as they silently stood next to each other and took in the beautiful, flower-filled view.

"You know this was a good idea for all of us to get away together. The past few months have been hard on Dee because of her dad's illness and recent loss. Ellie needed a break from the modeling agency she's trying to create, and well, I just needed some time off!"

"I know what you mean, Leena. I believe fun-time recharges us. Let's go see what Dee is whipping up for lunch in the kitchen. She sure has been in there for a long time. She has kicked me out at least three times!"

❖

Ellie grabbed a spoon and scooped out some sauce from the pot just as Dee walked back into the kitchen. "Oooooh yummy, this is goooood."

Dee's slap almost knocked the spoon out of Ellie's hand.

"Hey what was that for?"

"You are cheating. You're supposed to wait until I'm done!" Dee chided.

"So is lunch ready or what?" piped in Aggie as she walked into the kitchen.

"Gosh, none of you know patience," Dee said with a sigh. "Yes, lunch is ready."

Everyone laughed at Dee's exasperated tone which she then changed into a butler's announcement. "Lunch will be served in the veranda promptly at 12. Would anyone like some ice tea with their meal?"

❖

Leena stretched, and yawned loudly. After the meal, the girls decided to sprawl out in the wicker sofas throughout the sun room. No one moved much for about an hour.

Leena interrupted the silence.

"Anyone want iced tea?" Without waiting for a reply, she got up and darted into the house.

Dee looked at the sky and began to wonder about her dad. She was lost in her thoughts and didn't realize that her questions were no longer in her head but had escaped her mouth.

"I wonder if he really is in heaven."

"Oh I'm sure he is…without a doubt."

Dee was startled by Aggie's reply. "Did I say that out loud?"

"Did you say what out loud?" Leena asked as she walked back in with the tray.

"I was thinking about my dad and was wondering if there is really a heaven and stuff like that."

"Well, I think there is and I believe he is there because he was a good man." Ellie said and continued, "Yup, your dad was a saint. He always took such good care of all of you guys after your mom passed away."

Leena passed out the drinks and sat back down.

"Do you really think we get into heaven because of the good that we do? I mean, think about it. Most of us have screwed up royally at some point or another. Shouldn't that count against us? How much good do we have to do to make up for all of those things we did wrong, purposely?" The questions came out quickly, one after the other. Leena finally paused long enough for Ellie to jump in.

"Well I'm going to hell," she broke in sarcastically.

"Nah, you're Saint Ellie," Leena said with a sly smile.

"Come on, seriously," Dee continued, "when I think about all of Leena's questions, I wonder if she's right. What if you can't make it in by being good? I mean what is good? Who determines what is being good? Us…heck, our motto is 'if it feels good, go for it.' "

Everyone looked at Dee. Ellie rolled her eyes and said, "Oh boy, Aggie, you got her started."

Dee ignored the comment. "This is important to me. I keep wondering about what happens after you die. Is this it? I mean, do I get to see my dad once again."

Dee's heartfelt questions brought on an awkward silence.

Aggie finally spoke up. "A week before your dad went into a coma, I went to visit him. He said 'out of all my daughter's friends, you always seem to be the happy go-lucky one, no matter what is going on.' He wanted to know why. I explained to him how I had finally solved my heart issues. Although I kept myself busy by doing different things, I found that nothing kept me happy. You know my story. I got married, it didn't work out. I got divorced. I then decided to put all that energy into climbing up the corporate ladder. I became really good at what I do, but at the end of the day when I come home to an empty apartment, then what? I have good friends, but you all have your own lives. I vacation whenever I want with whomever I want. I go out to dinner at a whim, catch Broadway shows, go shopping, etc. etc., but eventually it's back to the same thing, day in and day out."

Aggie's face lit up as she continued. "Your dad smiled and asked me if I had found religion. I told him that I had found something better and of course you know Dee's dad, he loves stories. He asked me to tell him everything, down to the last detail."

Aggie glanced at Dee. "Your father was amazing that way. Where others would become bored to death with details, he relished every tidbit."

Dee smiled, "You're right."

"I told him that I was flipping through the channels one night and I came across this woman whose question caught my attention. She asked 'are you really getting what you want from life?' I began to listen to her and she was just, so down to earth, and not like most of those people on TV that scream at you. It was the first time I heard anyone refer to God as someone real and tangible. She said that God was interested in me, in every aspect of my life, and most importantly, was concerned about my happiness. This struck a chord with me because, although I have acquired lots of things, and have what most consider a good life, you know good job, house, family and friends that love me; I knew in my heart that I wasn't entirely happy. There was always something missing inside."

"So you became one of those Jesus freaks?" Ellie asked but was quickly interrupted by Dee.

"I really want her to finish telling me what she told dad, ok?"

Ellie slumped into her chair and gestured to Aggie to continue.

"She asked what if everything was taken away from you, then what? Most of us would want to crumble up and die because we have a tendency to define our worth by how much we have, but think about it, when we leave this world, we leave with nothing."

She focused back on Dee.

"Your dad pointed towards himself at this point and said…'Look at me. I have had everything in life but now I feel like I have nothing. Laying here in this bed gives you a lot of time to think and take inventory on your life.' I continued my story and told him how this woman explained that having stuff does not define you. Where your heart is, does. Our actions are basically the outward display of whatever is going on in our heart. We always want more because the only one who can fill that restless, empty spot is God. Now, before you jump down my throat about religion, hear me out. It's not about religion, it's about relationship. She challenged me at the end of the program, and I took her up on that challenge because at that point I didn't feel like I had anything to lose. Heck I tried everything else….why not this?"

"Ok so out with it, what did you try?" All the girls gave Ellie the sideways, *cut it out* look. After a moment Aggie continued.

"She asked, how can anyone say that something does not work

or how God does not exist, and yet live in blind certainty when it comes to one's daily life. We believe or are certain that we will wake up the next morning, when there is no guarantee. Have you ever stopped to think about the complexity of your body and how your organs work? You trust it will work, although you can't see how it works. We call that science. She called it a miracle. How can we be certain of everything we cannot see inside of us, but readily dismiss the existence of God? What she said next made me wonder. 'If everything else hasn't changed your troubled heart, perhaps it's time you gave the creator of your body and soul a real chance; not a halfhearted one. I challenge you to challenge the reality of God by proving that He doesn't exist. You can't say something doesn't exist unless you've verified it. Too many people go by what other people say. Don't be a follower. Why don't you find out for yourself?' She then asked us to repeat a simple prayer, and said we should find a good church, which by the way, I did.

To answer your question Ellie, again, it's not about religion, it's about relationship. My relationship with God is as real as my relationship with you. He is real -- as real as you're sitting across from me. I know what you are thinking. I can't see Him. I can't see wind, Ellie, but I can feel it. The wind is real. God is real, and I feel Him. My heart became complete and I finally found hope when I decided to give God a chance."

She then focused back on Dee and took one of her hands. "I probably should have told you earlier but with all the craziness, it was hard to get some quiet time with you. Your dad said that same prayer that afternoon with me at the hospital, and that's why I said and believe and know without a shadow of a doubt that he's in heaven."

Your Heart Lesson

You must be wondering, why there's the need to cover spirituality? No heart journey would be complete without it. So far we've journeyed through the physical, social and emotional. However, the spiritual is the foundation that sustains all the rest. Without it, you will remain incomplete. Ultimately, your belief system is what provides sustenance and guidance. When that part of your life is missing, it creates an imbalance. Any changes you make becomes a temporary pattern. You become known as the person who constantly says you're going to change but never do. To have no spirituality is like being a table with three legs. You will always wobble.

Throughout our lives our hearts have been broken because of disappointments either by others or because of choices we've made. We often carry scars and our hearts become limited. What is wrong with scars? Scars can remain open or closed. Open scars continuously hurt. (Ever get salt in an opened wound?) Closed scars leave their mark. The area remains disfigured. Although time makes one forget the intensity of the hurt, it never erases it completely. The problem with heart scars is that no one can see them, that is, no one but you, and God.

The reason why there are many women who have heart issues is because they think that they can handle it or are convinced that eventually they will go away. However, if we really take a hard, close, and honest look within ourselves, most times the reason why we feel so incomplete is because we know that deep down inside, we can't fix ourselves. It's something that's beyond us. We'll even acknowledge that a miracle needs to happen in our heart, but we'd rather dismiss the existence of God and cling to the tangible.

There is nothing wrong with seeking out tangible things,

however, everything that is tangible eventually ceases to exist, and that includes your outer shell; the person you see in the mirror. When it comes to the final hour, it's just you, your heart, and whatever your beliefs are.

What is your belief system today? Does it provide enough sustenance to keep your heart filled with the positive and good, despite what's happening in the world…your world? If you experienced trauma or loss, does it help you get to a place of peace and comfort?

Here are a few examples of the value of having a belief system.

Situation:
Every day is the same old thing and I can't get out of this rut.

Negative:
Nothing changes. No matter what I try. I'll never change.

Counteract:
I can do all things I put my mind to. This is a temporary situation.

Positive A: You can change.

When you incorporate a belief system, it will provide a positive push towards anything in life. As a matter of fact, God encourages us to live life to the fullest, in all aspects.

Any time you initiate change, you'll notice that people you thought were friends will question or discourage you. They'll say things like "I don't think that will work" or "Why change a good thing?" Keep in mind that what is good for them may not necessarily be good for you.

For change to remain a constant you need a strong foundation. You may have a weak or non-existant foundation because it was cracked or excavated out from under you because of your past. It's essential that you start to lay down the right groundwork before you start to build on it.

If you always wondered why you have trouble with commitment or keeping promises to yourself or others, it's because your foundation is flawed. The wonderful thing about God is that He *always* sees your potential. He knows (not thinks) that you can do so many great things in life.

Imagine trying to live up to His expectations knowing that the Creator of the universe knows you can achieve whatever wonderful dream you set your heart to, and has promised that He'll be with you in your journey.

Positive Actions will shut down
halfhearted changes,
and will <u>establish an unshakeable foundation</u>.

Situation:
I always feel like there is something missing in my life.

Negative:
I guess I'll have to deal with that feeling for the rest of my life.

Counteract:
I can change this emptiness if I choose the right spiritual source.

Positive A: You can free yourself from those empty feelings.

What is your outlet when you feel empty inside?

Do you search for a new partner or go to the next party? Both of these things are not bad things, but they will eventually cause problems in your life when they are the continual answers to your empty feelings.

Maybe you bury those emotions with the bottle or by eating, and have begun to realize that you no longer have control and cannot stop. The alcohol or the chocolate cake has become your faithful, daily companion, and provides the comfort you so much desire.

No matter how you choose to fill in the gaps, those things eventually become detrimental habits. Overindulgence in the drinking and eating department will eventually kill your self-esteem because alcohol and being overweight have the same end result -- depression.

Each of us has a spirit and that spirit knows that there is more to life than what we see. You will always feel like something is missing until you discover your place in the Kingdom and how unbelievably loved you are by God. When God becomes an intricate part of your life, you finally understand your value, and why life was so empty without Him. You will finally feel whole and complete.

Positive Actions will shut down
the empty feelings
and will <u>promote the sense of wholeness</u>.

Situation:
I live in a house full of people but always feel lonely.

Negative:
There must be something wrong with me because I should not feel this way.

Counteract:
I can stop this lonely feeling when I accept and recognize I'm never alone.

Positive A: You are never alone.

Some of us experience a deep ache inside and constantly feel lonely even though we're married, have children, or have lots of people who love us. A lot of us try to bury that feeling and become accessible to anyone and everyone as a way of running away from dealing with deep loneliness. We say yes to whatever is asked of us. After a while, we feel depleted because we give and give until we have nothing left to give. Busyness becomes our daily routine in order to shut out that ache. The ache, however, will not go away because it's your spirit that's longing to connect with God's spirit.

It's a wonderful feeling when we connect with someone else. We wish it could last forever. However, the harsh reality is that people will, at some point, let you down. We are only human, after all. God, however, is constant and will never let you down. When you decide to connect with God, you will discover that what He offers you is constant love and acceptance. His love is unwavering, and forever and He promises to always be with you, no matter what.

Positive Actions will shut down the lonely feelings, and will <u>promote a sense of well-being</u>.

In all fairness, don't you owe it to yourself to continue down your path of exploration and answer all of the hard questions that have unsettled your heart? Life is about more than what you see. It's about more than being physically healthy, socially inclined, and emotionally balanced. Life is a spiritual road that purposely crosses the paths of others. It is no coincidence that you're reading this book. Whether you believe it or not, this book and the words you are reading now were written for you, for this specific moment and have a specific purpose. These words are part of God's comfort and healing. They are also part of God's plan.

This book, thus far, has been about choices. Once again you have the power to choose. However, before you decide to dismiss what you've read, make sure you answer the hard questions.

Why should you?

It will be the only way to look back and say, I turned over every stone that I was supposed to and left nothing to question.

Whenever you make a decision in life, especially the tough decisions, it's important to feel like you have tried everything before you walk away. Otherwise you'll always wonder about the 'what ifs.'

Your Heart and Spirituality Assignment

Your life is not complete until it includes core beliefs that provide you balance. It's important to answer the hard, heart questions and become spiritually in-tuned with the gal within.

- Think about your spiritual beliefs. Do you have any? If your belief system is non-existent, inconsistent (erratic) or weak (ineffective):
  o Write down why you don't have a belief system.

- o Write down why you have an inconsistent belief system.
- o Or, write down why you have a weak one at the present time.

Before you dismiss anything with spirituality, you owe it to yourself to explore and prove whether it's something you truly do not need. Approach this as a relationship with God, not religion. Begin by talking to Him just as you would talk to a friend. Don't be afraid to tell Him the truth and how you really feel.

For the Explorer

If you desire to continue to change, and want to establish a good and solid belief system, I extend an invitation to you to receive God's gift, the Lord Jesus as your personal Savior.

Sincerely pray this simple prayer below if you are ready to accept this gift.

Salvation Prayer:

Lord Jesus I receive You as Lord and Savior and accept your gift of salvation. Forgive me of my sins. Thank you for your sacrifice and accepting me into Your kingdom. Amen.

Yes it is as simple as that. If you have said this prayer, these next steps are very important.

Find a church that teaches the Word of God and that can help you grow in your relationship with Jesus Christ. It may take some time to find a church and church family that you feel open and comfortable with. However, being surrounded by those who can encourage and strengthen you in your new walk with Jesus is worth every minute.

For those who do not wish to pursue …

If you decided not to take this step, my hope is that you will not stop your search for spiritual significance, and that this chapter has motivated you to continue to ask yourself the hard, heart questions.

Stop
Ignoring
Me

Story Update

Dee finally opened up her own hair salon and had to hire two additional people after a couple of months to keep up with the influx of new and prior clients. She still struggles once in a while with her feelings of inadequacy but quickly reminds herself of all that she has accomplished, despite past fears and loss. Dee feels like she is finally being true to herself in all areas of her life.

Ellie just launched her first advertising campaign for LEAD Modeling Agency. She chose the first initials of each of her friends, including her own. It was her way of saying thank you for their support during her time of change. Ellie battles with her past from time to time, but her new spiritual belief-system reminds her that she is a valuable individual, no matter what others may think.

Leena's husband filed for a divorce as he believed that there was no point to continue the marriage. Leena decided to go back to school and is majoring in psychology. It is her hope that she can help others that have been abused by a partner. Leena volunteers at different women's shelters as a way to heal and cope with her past. She refuses to return to her prison of silence.

Aggie resigned from her marketing position and decided to partner with her cousin Ellie. The death of Dee's father made her take inventory of her own life. She realized that she wanted a slower-paced life. Aggie met someone special who respects and treats her like a queen. It was someone she had known for a long time, but her schedule didn't provide the right conditions for it to flourish.

All of the women in our story achieved some level of success, but it wasn't without a price. Each woman was required to take a hard look inside and decide what needed to change. As you know, some of those changes were no fun. As a matter of fact, some of those changes were downright painful. However, all of them chose to live life to their fullest, and they knew that they could not do so until adjustments were made in the way they thought and did things. They finally began to understand what authentic living means.

Did you know that there is a difference between living and existing? When you decide to live life in a substandard way, you exist. Existing is actually described as living on the minimum level. Unfortunately, many have chosen to live on the bare minimum emotionally for so long that they have gone into auto-pilot. Everything is routine in their daily lives and it has become quite comfortable. However, that comfort zone is shaken from time to time when they see the success of their friends or the growth of other people in their lives.

You may think there's nothing wrong with being comfortable where you are, but you should live in constant motion, and that motion should always be forward and/or upward.

Everything that you have learned so far has guided you towards self-love. Why is this so important? A person who doesn't love oneself can never fully love anyone else. You cannot give what you don't have. It is hard to love yourself especially when you hold on to the things that you have done in the past.

Some of you will say, you don't know how or you won't forgive yourself. You would rather hold onto your mistake. This will cause you to channel the dislike inward instead of acknowledging the wrong, repenting and moving on. To repent doesn't mean just to feel bad about it. It requires that you initiate change by making a U-turn away from the mistakes and move towards something better.

Here is where most fail. Many would rather moan, groan, complain, give up, and feel helpless, than do something that may be painful. It hurts to change, but when it's done for growth, the results cause you to love yourself. You finally start to enjoy who you are. It's an amazing, content-filled feeling.

All of these steps were necessary to help you begin to deal with the root of certain issues. Once you chose change, you began to see yourself in a different light. Who you see, this new woman was always there. All you needed to do was to take a good look inside to assess the damage.

It became a matter of choice before you willingly decided it was time to clean out the cobwebs, polish some fixtures, and perhaps even rearrange some furniture. You are like a house that has an assortment of rooms. Sometimes some of these rooms are locked tight, but it doesn't separate itself from the whole house. It does not create another house. It was always part of that structure and cannot be ignored forever. Eventually all the rooms need to be cleaned out.

If the reflection in your mirror asked you, "Where are you now in your journey?" What would you say?

Could you really answer that question honestly or would you hmm and haw in front of the mirror? Do you like where you're at right now?

The only person who can answer that is you and no one else. You're responsible and have the ownership to make your life the best that it can be. Your choices, whether they are emotional, physical, social, or spiritual, determine how you live. Bad choices reap a bad life. Good choices reap a good life. I am not saying that bad things do not happen to good people, but how you choose to handle the bad things in your life makes a world of a difference.

Why do you think certain people beat the odds with diseases? It's not luck. It is because, in most cases, they have aligned the four parts of their lives correctly. They became stubborn in their positive beliefs, even when those beliefs were contrary to what the doctors, science, society and common sense said.

Did you really dedicate the time and effort in the investment of self, or did you hope to find a quick fix in your present situation?

Let's review the seven points that were covered in the previous chapters. It will give you a chance to gauge where you are in your journey.

1. <u>Masks will hide the real you.</u>

Masks are not based on how you treat people, but how you show yourself to be. Naturally, you will treat your family differently than your co-workers, friends and acquaintances. However when you wear a mask, you make believe you're something you're not. No one wants to experience rejection. You want to be accepted. However, when the mask defines and dominates how you live, you are adding to the pain you're so desperately trying to avoid.

You create your own masks by the way you speak to yourself and of yourself. When you say things like "I'm not good enough," "I can't," "I'm stupid," "I'm fat," "I'm not beautiful," and other negative comments, you feed into your **K**ill **T**he **E**steem syndrome.

Do you still suffer from KTE? It's a pattern that can be spotted from a mile away. For example, a friend sees you and gives you a compliment on how beautiful you are. How do you respond? Is your answer still like this? "No I'm not" or "Do you need glasses?"

To accept a compliment doesn't mean conceit. It does mean that you're confident and comfortable in your skin. If you desire change, and if you desire to live a happier life, it's important that you learn to fix or remove the things that cause you to hide who you really are.

Perhaps you've discovered that when you decided not to address underlying issues, you essentially chose to live a lie. You live someone else's life and not your own. If you still live with a mask, remember that everyone gets to know the masked person who lives in fear, but never the person you really are.

2. <u>Fear will cause you to run inwardly</u>.

As you know, fear is something that everyone experiences. It is also an emotion that can rob you of your dreams, hopes and willingness to take risk. Fear can either hurt or protect you. People do great things even when they are afraid. If you ever ask those people who have overcome great obstacles in their lives how they did it, chances are that they will tell you that they did it despite of fear.

Fear has a way to make you run. You may not see your feet move when you look down, but if you'd take a peek inside yourself, you'd definitely see those feet zoom by.

Fear causes you to run away from your emotions. It'll make you think that you are safe in your run. Masks and fear go hand-in-hand. Whenever fear is present, it keeps you well hidden and away from anything that can change your life in a positive way.

What fears do you continue to have today? Do you feel that your fears still dominate your decisions in life?

If so, don't let fears in one part of your life become a false perception that you carry into all the other areas of your life. Don't let fear fill you with false beliefs about yourself. False beliefs will only create insecurity.

3. <u>Insecurity keeps you in constant doubt</u>.

Being unsure is normal, especially when you try anything new. The problem isn't in the uneasiness that you feel, it's in the intensity of the emotion and how often you experience it. Fear and insecurity go hand-in-hand. Fear fuels insecurity. In turn, insecurity will stop you from taking the risks necessary to go after your dreams.

Insecurity will not let you move forward physically, emotionally, socially and spiritually. It will limit you and exhaust you. When you live under constant limitations that are fueled by self-doubt, it will exhaust you because you are constantly second-guessing yourself.

Do you feel like you still battle with insecurities today? Have you taken the time to answer the whys?

Make it a goal to get underneath the problems that cause those insecure feelings and remind yourself over and over again, of all of the good qualities you possess.

4. <u>Appreciation of the good inside of you brings out your best</u>.

All of us have been born with certain talents. Did you know that you are not here on this earth by accident and that there is a plan and purpose for your life? You have something that you alone can contribute.

Your past mistakes do not forfeit your gift and your responsibility to share it.

We all have good inside of us. You possess great and wonderful gifts that God has given you. Having these good qualities doesn't always mean you will make right choices—and this is OK. However, when you don't take time to become aware of the good inside yourself, you don't live your best and you don't fully experience and share your gifts.

Your goodness and gifts will remain undiscovered until you get rid of the guilt.

Do you still feel guilty about something that happened to you in the past? Does it stop you from seeing the good that you possess?

You cannot undo what is done, but you can make sure you don't repeat the same mistakes. You can forge a new path and future because of the power behind the new choices that you can make.

5. <u>Wise choices will change your life</u>.

Choice is always available to you. However, there are certain times when you may feel you don't have choices. There is never a situation where you have zero choices. Usually, you choose not to consider them because you don't like them for various reasons. When you feel like you have no choices, you have actually chosen not to do anything.

To make a choice can be hard at times, and the end result of making a choice usually requires change. If you are like most people, you don't like change. However, it is a necessary and vital part of life, especially if you want to move forward and see positive results in your life. Life is about choices. How you make them and what you choose determines the outcome of your life.

Do you still make the same choices or have you started to change your decision-making habits?

If you base decisions on the mental note that nothing great will ever happen to you, then it never will. If something in your life hasn't changed that needs to, it may be because you have continued to make the same bad choices. Get out of that habit and create a new habit.

When making choices in your life, weigh all your decisions, enlist the help of a friend if need be, and look at all the possible outcomes before you make a final choice.

6. <u>Maintain healthy friendships and promote personal growth</u>.

It has been said that you are who you keep company with. People will identify your character by the circles of friends with whom you associate. A lot of people don't care what others think, however, the influence of friendship usually contributes significantly to one's character.

Friendship is a crucial part of your social structure. Your friends may even include members within your family circle. Depending on the closeness of these relationships, it can have a positive or negative impact in your life. These relationships can either push you to become a better individual or help kill your dreams and esteem.

What type of friendships do you continue to nurture? Do you feel like they help or hinder your personal growth?

Your relationships should be two-sided. For the most part, the contributions into the relationship should be positive from both ends. Sometimes you will outgrow a friendship. These are known as seasonal friendships. Learn not to hold on to relationships that you need to let go.

Remember, you are like a flower, and will not grow as long as you have weeds in your garden.

7. <u>Your spiritual-belief system provides sustenance and guidance</u>.

Your spiritual-belief system should be the foundation that sustains all of the areas of your life. When it is missing, you will limp through life.

A woman who understands and accepts how God sees her, experiences a freedom that most women desire. They understand who they are, move forward despite their fears, overcome their insecurities, recognize their potential, weigh all of their choices, and surround themselves with people who build them and help promote their dreams. You too can achieve these things. It is not impossible. Nothing is impossible with God.

Spiritual emptiness is the driving factor that keeps you from being your true self. When you are spiritually void inside, your perceptions are based on what others have told you instead of what God says. You measure yourself against society's standards, what others think or based on your past history. As long as you do not discover your value in Christ, you will not know what true freedom is (in every sense of the word).

How do you feel about your spiritual life today? Do you still feel like there's something missing?

When you see yourself through the eyes of God, it is the most powerful eye-opener you can have in your life. God expects you to live life in excellence. His desire is that you live a happy and fulfilled life. However, you will never understand this until you experience a relationship with Christ.

All of us willingly rely on people we don't know or even see every single day, and yet, when it comes to God, a lot of us have silent reservations. Those who claim not to believe in God or organized religion are quick to denounce a belief based on observation and is very seldom based on experience.

Why is experience so important?

When you participate, not just observe life's events, it actually teaches you, and what you learn affects you. It is so much easier in today's age to intellectualize everything, especially religion. Yet, God is not about religion. Man created religion. God just wants a relationship with you -- that's all He ever wanted. He understands the importance of connection and the effect it has on us all when nurtured.

Trust, belief, expectation, and sureness are part of our daily lives, but they only grow if we are consistent in our daily encounters with each one.

When someone lacks faith, it is an indicator that they have had limited experience in a relationship with God.

Denial or no faith is a sign that a person knows of God but has no relationship experience.

Faith in God is not intellectual. It's an individual, spiritual and relational experience.

It's in the relational experience with God that you experience positive expectation. However, living in positive expectation can never be heightened if you do not understand the principle of being able to do all things. Only God can bring this affirmation of truth to your life.

The knowledge of positive expectation brings contentment and contentment is the result of choice. Positive Expectation is the end product of right-thinking, a grateful heart, understanding your value and living in expectation for something greater.

Perhaps you have not reached the point of real change yet in your life. The problem with most of us is that we want a quick fix for everything, and we'll skip, skim or find the fastest way to it. Truth is that there is no quick fix when it comes to change and healing. Mending will never happen overnight. It requires constant and consistent work. No one likes to hear that. However, the truth is always hard to hear and even harder to apply.

What decision have you made today? Will you continue to ignore yourself, or will you step up to the plate and stick with change and continually remove the bad, and consistently incorporate the good?

It's important you get this. One read of this book will not change you. It can only give you a jump start. You need to choose to follow through on everything, even when your life feels grand and you're back on track. Don't let your comfort zone keep you at the same place. Bookmark my website and read and watch inspirational messages that will keep you motivated, inspired and grounded.

Don't lose momentum once you walk away from this book. What keeps life's lessons fresh and in constant motion is to share your life-changing discoveries with those around you. It will motivate others to want change.

To share what you have learned also holds you at a certain standard because it will make you accountable to others. This means that other people, including those close to you, will raise the bar as far as their expectations of you. This is not a bad thing. It should push you to strive for better.

Be patient and believe that change will come. It may never happen the way you want it to and will probably happen differently than what you expect. However, you should learn to wait in forward motion.

What does it mean to wait in forward motion?

It means exactly that…do while you wait. There may be certain things that you can't have right now. You have to wait. But that doesn't mean you sit idly by. You still have to consistently and constantly move yourself forward in your journey. You may not get what you want because it is not available to you at the moment, or because you aren't ready to receive it. The beauty in the wait is the discovery if what you want, is really what you should have.

It's not enough to believe that change will happen while you wait. You also have to do while you believe. You may believe you deserve a higher-paying job and there is nothing wrong with that. The question is, what are you doing while you wait to get that higher-paying job?

Forward motion while you wait requires an action from you. Let's face it there are certain things in your life that just won't get resolved overnight. Remember these are actions required from you to promote change. To move forward, you may be required to:

1. Forgive and let go. Forgiveness frees you because as long as you hold a grudge, the person that wronged you keeps control over your life.

2. Voice your hurt. No one is a mind reader and you can't fix what you don't voice or acknowledge.

3. Get help. There are just certain things you can't fix by yourself.

4. Find accountability. At times you require someone to keep you accountable in your change from a weakness or in your reach for a goal.

5. Face it. Don't ignore the issue. Whatever the mistake or issue is, know that you are human and you have a God that says you have another chance. It's your choice to accept that chance or not.

6. Set a plan. If you do not see your vision or dream before you, it's hard to remain consistent, especially after failure.

Love, strength, and beauty are the discoveries you make while on this journey of authentic, balanced living. Real living is when you choose to experience life to the fullest. You do not ignore the things that need change. You address problems as they come. You seek peace and fulfillment the right way. You promote your well-being and maintain a balanced healthy life physically, emotionally, socially and spiritually.

When you learn to live this way, everything that you build up on the inside, will eventually manifests itself in your life on the outside. Your attitude, demeanor, stance, character, and basically everything about you, becomes appealing and contagious.

Don't fall into the trap of a motionless life. It is boring and empty. Listen to the woman inside of you, and never lead her back into that desperate place where she cries out again, *STOP IGNORING ME.*

Beauty Within Self

The reflection of beauty

within self

slowly unfolds

for all to see

Enveloping outwardly

in radiance

that overflows

Catching the eye

that which cannot be hidden

for all to behold

Author's Note:

It is my heart's desire that this book has opened a new door for you and has propelled you to journey and see yourself in a different light.

As you read along, you've discovered or identified certain things that have become obstacles in your life; running and hiding, insecurity, lack of vision, poor or no friendships, the weight of choices, your point of reference and your validity. Your world will always be rocked if you do not have a firm foundation or belief system. My hope is that you will continue to balance your life and listen to the woman inside you who needs some attention from time to time.

If this book has impacted your life, please do not hesitate to contact me at www.rozhumphreys.com. I would love to hear about it.

Bunches of blessings!

About the Author

Roz Humphreys is an author, teacher and motivational speaker. For over 30 years, Roz has encouraged women of all ages to recognize their value and potential. Her no-nonsense attitude laced with Latin love has steered and encouraged women towards wholeness. Her educational resources and women's forums continue to motivate women to pursue their passion and purpose.

Roz and her husband Richard are native New Yorkers who have embraced New England's beauty and charm. They have 2 young adult daughters.

Roz is also the author of:

- Get Dressed! Life has stripped you…NOW WHAT?,
- Get UNSTUCK and Spirit GAL Hear!

The Story Behind the Book

People often want to know what motivated me to write something. This book was part of my own journey of rediscovery. I kind of lost myself after I became a mom. I was so over-focused and over-dedicated solely to my family that along the way I lost my identity. Now don't misunderstand. It is commendable for a woman to pour into her children, but my family became my all. I forgot that I had an assignment to fulfill, and that in me was deposited such an incredible treasure that God wanted to use. There were a lot of gals counting on me, just like there are a lot of people counting on you that are outside of your immediate family structure.

I struggled with a lot of the stuff that was talked about in this book. It was written after I emerged from a dark period in my life almost 20 years ago. I became lost within myself and there were some awesome friends that came along side me to help me through. These were seasonal friendships, and I will always be grateful for how they helped me see what I couldn't. I lost sight of the reality of who I was, not the potential of who I could be, but who I was. Even though I was broken, it didn't change the reality of my value as an individual and as the daughter of The King.

You might be asking yourself why I finally released this book now. It is very simple. It is because you needed it now. This book was written for you. It humbles me every time I think about that.

My deepest desire is that you discover all the great things about yourself and that you walk into the confidence of your destiny. Why? It is the place where you will feel fulfilled. It will put a skip to your step, a leap to your heartbeat and a rhythm to how you face life. It's how I feel each time I sit and write; each time I outline a class; and each time I have the awesome opportunity to teach or speak.

This book was about, "Yup, been there and done that, but it will and can get better." It will and can get better. In spirit, I walk along with you. I prayed for your emergence. And…I prayed for your healing. Big…big…hug.

www.ingramcontent.com/pod-product-compliance
Lightning Source LLC
LaVergne TN
LVHW051103080426
835508LV00019B/2039